Now You Know

The Case Against God in America

Virginia E. Connolly

Contents

Dedication

I dedicate this book to God, who inspired me to write it. On behalf of my children and grandchildren [including those I've adopted]. My Nieces and Nephews and their Little ones. And my siblings. May we fight to pass down what was passed down to us. True love of God, Family and Country.

Acknowledgment

I would like to acknowledge Our Founding Fathers, who graced us with Liberty. My Father who introduced me to both God and Politics. A man who saw what was coming back in the 60s that those entering into the political area wanted to change America into a Socialist form of government. But told me I wouldn't live to see it but My Grandchildren would. How I wish he'd been wrong. I am watching it play out before my very eyes. And I really do not accept what I am seeing. My grandchildren deserve better than this.

But because of Him, I'm still willing to fight for what I know is right! For my grandchildren and for what Our Founding Fathers believed we could be. It's the America I want to hand down to them. "A Constitutional Republic, if we can keep it." as Benjamin Franklin forewarned. Well, Mr. Franklin millions of us are willing to fight to Keep what You gave to us. God bless you, sir. I also want to acknowledge those who encouraged me as I finally set about to fulfill my dream of becoming a published writer.

About the Author

Virginia Connolly, known by her friends as Ginny, is from the Baby Boomer generation. Born and raised in Philadelphia, where she was introduced to the political area at the young age of 10 thanks to her father's involvement. She spent the first half of her adult life in Bucks County Pa where she raised her two children and finally retired to her beloved Jersey Coastal area. A woman of strong conviction regarding her Faith in God and her Dedication to Him and The Constitution of The United States believes God belongs in government. Always dreaming of becoming a Writer and finally having the time to live out that dream, this is Virginia's first Book with the hopes of many to follow.

Chapter One

Court Challenges against the First Amendment

You know, I have come to the conclusion that the most difficult task in writing is finding the perfect opening sentence! And that if you let it, it can paralyze you from the beginning. It's a challenge I've struggled with for decades. Not years. Decades. But no more. Especially when I hear my oldest grandson, a graduate of Penn State University who now has the complete knowledge of the intricacies of how the entire body works and the job of each inner connecting element and how they are designed to work together for the good of the whole. Yet when we talk about the government, the one designed to work for his benefit, he has to admit to me; he has no knowledge of these matters! And I can only ask why is that? And can only reach one conclusion; since it is our educational system that is managed, funded and run by our federal government that denies this knowledge. It must be intentional on their part.

So that, my friends, is why I am finally inspired to begin this. What I hope will serve as an informative book. Realizing it is primarily for those who "have ears to hear." And a willingness to learn and know what they were denied! An opportunity to think things through and make a choice.

I pray what you read will be inspiring, insightful, and filled with thought-provoking knowledge. Knowledge is meant to challenge your way of thinking; with regards to how you choose to use the most wonderful gift ever given to the common man. The right to listen, think on and ultimately cast a ballot for who should represent you in our government. Instead of being forced to live under the ruling of the Monarchs as all our ancestors were subject to; until one of them made their way to the shores of America.

Knowledge, I believe, is much needed in this next crucial general election. Because many already in government are determined to once again present to The People candidates that pose no threat to the little world within our nation's government they have been successful in creating. A little world where they have the ultimate say over the will and lives of the people. And will not tolerate anyone who disagrees with and dares to challenge what they are doing. Make no mistake; this next general election will determine whether or not this Constitutional Republic [as Benjamin Franklin described it when asked by a citizen as he was departing from the Constitutional Convention held in Philadelphia] survives. And continues to be a nation of The People by The People for The People.

My primary goal here is to reintroduce you to knowledge and references you may have forgotten or never really knew. Knowledge about our nation. How it was established, designed with the commoner in mind. Fashioned to give that commoner the voice they never had before; concentrating on articles of the First Amendment that are meant to be read and taken together as one. Instead of having been pitted against one another for more than a decade. I am using knowledge taken from Scripture, Our Declaration of Independence, and Our Constitution. Documents that are two very important pieces of one whole. Words fifty-six men struggled to develop into a penned declaration severing all ties from the most powerful Empire at the time. And to justify to the rest of the established world, why they were considering such a thing. And once that was accomplished, how they were going to set about the experiment of establishing, creating and governing a new country.

Something that had never been attempted before. But The primary reason why I stress reading them combined, despite having been written separately, is for the full understanding of the very purpose of their existence. But unfortunately, something very few American citizens seldom do. If they bother to read them at all! It will also touch on the discussions presented for consideration, Our Founding Fathers conveyed to each other, as well as to members of the colonies, via letters, now commonly referred to as The Federalist Papers. All of which were taken into serious consideration and debate as they embarked on that monumental task no man had ever attempted to do before. A nation guided under the principles that John Carver referenced when the first of the pilgrims anchored on the northeastern shores of The Atlantic Ocean back in 1620. When we Honor and respect the one True King, we need no other to rule over us.

I also know some of the words you will read are definitely inspired words from God. Since I lack the knowledge, insight or wisdom to have come up with some of what my own hand penned! And is presenting to you for your consideration. What I wish to convey, I firmly believe, is shared in the hearts and minds of millions of American citizens. What in God's name has happened to our nation? When did everything go so wrong? Is it really too far gone to even survive? Going no further before reminding you, in Luke 18:27 [NIV], Jesus replied, "What is impossible with man is possible with God. And again, in Matthew 19:26 [NIV], Jesus looked at them and said, "With man, this is not possible, but with God, all things are possible.

Fifty-six well-read men formed this great nation we live in. Men with enough sense to heed words written long ago. The Bible is one of their primary sources. The book that records the rise and fall of the Jewish people. Along with the details of who'd succeeded in overpowering and enslaving them over centuries. The self-written accounts of their repeated cycles of sin and failure. Of turning away from their Creator. Despite His numerous warnings of what such an act would bring upon them. He had made it perfectly clear His decrees, commands and statutes would lead to peace and prosperity as long as they were honored and upheld. Which they failed to do. Time and time again. Followed by the long, arduous, redemptive path back to what they had thrown away. Personally, I give the Jewish people an enormous amount of credit for admitting and recording their failures. Done for the sole purpose of sparing future generations how not to repeat their mistakes. That is real humility on full display!

So let us, if we are willing, take a look back to when we, as a nation, began to drift away from the philosophy those fifty-six men studied, learned from and believed was the only foundation to guarantee the survival of this nation they created. When they dared to declare to the world, we're going to follow God's commands and decrees. Place our trust in Him. Rely on His wisdom instead of our own limited line of thinking. Never having cause to doubt, He will keep his promises to bless us. Permit us to prosper. When exactly did we take that first step, strayed away from those biblical, philosophical foundations they'd painstakingly laid down on parchment, onto the path that leads to the fall? That could bring about the destruction and ultimate demise of The Greatest Experiment mankind ever dared to imagine!

The most unfortunate of realities, the most difficult to admit, is that we as a culture started allowing a few unelected people to impose opinions that led to living under unconstitutional rulings. Men who'd been positioned within the highest courts of our Judicial Branch, who'd rendered decisions in favor of an individual person. In all such cases, presenting demands that challenged our Christian-Judeao values. Our constitutional right to religious freedom; as well as the right to openly speak about those beliefs, anywhere in the public square. Choosing not to challenge those judicial decrees in favor of one citizen or group with a different belief system. That very first case: A person who opposed something most Americans had no problem with. In fact, something millions embraced as a shared tradition. One that had united us, as well as setting us apart from the rest of the world. The Principle that makes us The Shining City on the Hill. For all the world to see. The people who look to and honor God and, therefore, have no reason or need for a human King.

The Case in point that changed everything. A case that began in the Courts in New York State, where self-proclaimed communist parents resided. Believers in communism who found it offensive that their son was being subjected and forced to listen [not participate but listen] as his classmates recited a simple prayer before beginning the school day. For those who don't know what I'm referring to, it's the Supreme Court Case [dating back to 1962] identified as Engel vs. Vitale. The Case and Ruling that took us down the path away from honoring and acknowledging Our Creator. Our one true God. The act that denied generations of children from starting their day thinking about God. A fact I sadly know many in this world throughout all of time will choose never to acknowledge. The very existence of One True God.

Here are the words those parents found so offensive. And insisted their son never be forced to hear. It is known as The Regents Prayer. How children in America began their day of learning in our public schools, until June of 1962.

"Almighty God, we acknowledge our independence of Thee, and we beg Thy blessings upon us, our parents, our teachers, and our country."

The High Court of the State of New York was presented with The Case, on behalf of the son of Steven Engle, against William Vitale [president of the local school board], that court did not agree with the arguments their lawyers presented. The decision the New York Court rendered was based on the fact that The Prayer was voluntary and did, in fact, promote the free exercise of religion, which the court rightfully determined is also protected under the First Amendment: guaranteed freedom of speech. The New York's High Court also disagreed and that their argument fell short in proving that such a prayer was, in fact, the establishment of a nationwide government-preferred religion, being forced upon all of the citizens. The Engel's refused to accept that decision. A verdict strongly in line with the aforementioned First Amendment, intended to protect every child in the public school system of America. As well as the children in the public school their son attended. The Engel's challenged the very freedom of every child and the parents' of every child in America. Opposed to the Constitutional Right, American citizens have to worship their God anywhere and everywhere; in the manner they choose. As well as attacking and designating where the Engels believed the right to free speech could, in fact, be practiced. When the First Amendment was put in place to sanction all speech. And that is to be tolerated and accepted anywhere and everywhere. Just as all citizens are free, to choose not to participate, listen or engage in, according to personal preference, is equally protected under that First Amendment! In America no citizen was ever to be subjected to being silenced. The Founding Fathers placed such importance on those two rights that they are the first clearly specified rights of our amendments. Deemed to be of the highest importance and protected by all who would be elected to public office.

The Engel's refused to accept the High Court of New York's verdict. Not interested in the least at being tasked or forced to consider the rights, opinions or desires of anyone else in our nation; not just those who chose to live in New York State. Clearly, they and a few others who agreed with their cause to abolish and stop prayer from being recited in school hated the very mention of God. And were determined to impose the communist mindset of where they'd fled, denying such a freedom to those who did not share their belief. Or position with regards to the matter of God's existence or importance in one's life.

The Engels urged their attorneys to present the case to the highest Court in Our Land, The Supreme Court, insisting the only acceptable decision was to end school prayer in America, once and for all.

Now, despite the Supreme Court hearing the same strong arguments as the High Court of the State of New York, which upheld the rights of our First Amendment rights to religious freedom along with free speech, The Supreme Court, in a 6-1 decision, overturned the decision of New York Court, ruling instead in favor of the defendant.

Six of the seven men sitting on that court found a way to agree with the Engels. Personally, I can't help but wonder how many of them shared their opinion. And embraced the opportunity to deny the existence of God. Unwilling to accept the suggestion of a Supreme Being. Who had more power, authority and wisdom than they.

Somehow, those six men determined the humble words that make up the Regents Prayer did, in fact, violate the establishment clause of the First Amendment. And that reciting the prayer somehow constituted the establishment of a preferred religion. Let that stew for a minute and see if you can agree with such an outlandish concept! A verdict, it is worthy to note some scholars argue, changed the balance between governmental power and individual liberty. By limiting the power of the state governments. As it struck down the individual states' authority to conduct and implement the school district's curriculum within the borders of the individual school boards across each state, as they saw fit. And in accordance with the residents of said districts.

Mind you it is the residents of each county, city, district, and state that pay school taxes. The very funds used to build and maintain those public school buildings. Not to mention employ the staff needed to run those schools. Not the federal government. And since The Constitution's design is meant to honor the very right of the residents in each of our states to govern in accordance with the wishes and needs that best suit their views and values, that ruling made that fact null and void. For those of you who do not know, The Federal Department of Education wasn't established until the presidency of Jimmy Carter in the 1970's. An expansion meant to continue to build on LBJ's goal of creating "The Great Society."

Something else that went unchallenged that should have been. For two reasons. The formulation of the Federal Department of Education was used to expand the federal government. And impose federal regulations that interfere with the decisions of each individual State regarding their public education policies. By imposing, along with their rules and regulations regarding the implementation of how the federal government's so-called "Free Lunch Program" was to be facilitated into the nation's schools. And mandating how our public schools should operate with regards to that program. That served as the beginning of the federal government's slow but steady, continuous takeover of our educational system. Again in direct violation of Our Constitution by interfering with the individual State's rights as protected under Our Constitution.

The Carter administration justified itself in order to establish a nationwide free lunch program for children in need. A very worthy cause that could have been handled differently. Since each state has in effect multiple programs, including a Food Stamp Program, to assist people in need. The federal government could have opted to reach out to Governors and work with each state that informed them of an excessive burden in caring for the poor and needy. Seeking a mutually agreed means to the solution, in the more rural areas. Instead of just expanding the federal government.

Mind you we are a generous nation of people always willing to help our fellow citizens who are down on their luck, facing unexpected hard times, and are in need of a hand up. Fully away "There but the grace of God." But over the years, the hand-up has evolved into a continuous handout. Creating a stagnant element within our society. Generations of welfare recipients are willing to be beholden to their government. Which in return must be beholden to the working class to meet such needs. Many American citizens find themselves in need during their lifetimes. I was one of them. But at some point we need to be a contributor to our society. Not just a taker.

Believe me when I say the so-called free lunch program expanded the federal government in ways you can not begin to imagine! Beginning with a massive amount of new government employees, that we are still paying for through salaries, benefits and pensions. Not to mention, the free lunch program was expanded to offer free lunch to students and staff members. I personally know of teachers who were in poverty-stricken areas of Philadelphia. Who spoke of the massive amounts of food thrown out every day the students didn't want or like what was offered? What our government does best: waste money.

Now my opinion is presented for your consideration. First, regarding the Engel vs Vitale decision. The individual rights and freedoms have been stripped away from all school-age children here in America since that decision was handed down. Their parents and the taxpayers, who happen to fund the school districts across our nation, have been ignored. As well as the authority of every governor and all local and state elected representatives to set the curriculum of the public education across their state is now dictated on the whims of the current federal administration. All totaling well into the millions of American citizens in the years since that 1962 decision. How wrong is that? Very!!!

Rights and freedoms of the people, that were meant to always be protected by our federal government, have been violated, trampled on and ignored, all to appease a communist couple residing in The State of New York sixty-odd years ago. Freedom of speech should never be denied. Especially when we, the people, hand over our hard-earned money in the form of taxes so our government can build and maintain our government facilities for us. Including our public schools, meant to be used to educate our children. Our future generations. For the guaranteed continuance of this great nation.

With regards to the matter of the so-called free lunch. Folks, nothing the government claims to supply is free. Our government is not a business. It does not have any real source of income. Other than the now heavily taxed American Citizen, on every level. That is how the government and its many projects are funded. Even in the most poverty-stricken areas of our nation, in reality, it would have been much more financially beneficial if parents and the PTA organizations had been presented with the option of making any form of contribution possible to alleviate a child from going hungry.

That way, even parents on assistance could have contributed by purchasing and donating a loaf of bread and a jar of peanut butter from the assistance they receive to help all children. After all, walking with God, we are reminded that when we have two of anything and see a person in need, we are to offer the extra we have.

Jesus told us the poor would always be with us. I believe it's God's way of making sure we are willing to share whatever He has graced us with!

Personally, I find the Supreme Court's ruling very ambiguous in nature. And have a difficult time aligning it up against their conclusion that voluntarily reciting The Regents Prayer is, in fact, a violation of the establishment clause. And is in some way an attempt at establishing a religion of any sort.

Was that ruling meant to imply acknowledging the existence of God in any government building as an attempt to establish a nationwide religion? Does it mean the reciting of any form of prayer in any government building is also an attempt to establish a nationwide religion? After all, it has been the practice of this nation to open each Congressional Session with a Prayer. Seeking God's guidance, wisdom and blessings as they gather to represent the interests of the people and perform the business of people. As our first elected representatives did. Just as those in attendance at those first meetings of delegates from the thirteen colonies did when they gathered in Independence Hall more than two hundred and fifty years ago.

I see a huge difference in acknowledging the existence of God from the attempt at establishing a "preferred governmental religion." That the people would be forced to finance and maintain. Which is what that clause was designed to avoid. That our newly formed Government not be permitted to do what good old Henry The Eighth did. When he established the Church of England with the attitude, "This is my kingdom, this will be my preferred religion, and I, your King and Ruler, because I can do whatever I choose. And no one can stop me. And you will pay heavily to support and maintain my religion! On top of supporting The Crown!"

Here is the first amendment to Our Constitution: Congress shall make no law respecting an establishment of religion, or prohibiting the free exercise thereof, or abridging the freedom of speech or of the press, and to petition the Government for a redress of grievances.

I don't see how allowing students in our public educational system, anywhere across this great nation, to recite that simple prayer voluntarily was, in fact, an intentional attempt to establish a preferred religion of any sort. Especially not one that would be imposed upon our nation. What I do see, however, is an attempt to limit, severely limit, where we, a free people, are permitted to express a belief in God. And practice our right to free speech on all subject matter, including religious beliefs.

I realize my thoughts are heavily influenced by the fact that my ancestors, on all sides of my heritage, came to this country from either England, Ireland or Scotland. All territories of the British Empire, meaning they were referred to as subjects, not citizens and were subjected to the rule of The Crown. Whomever that might be, and what they chose to leave. The first to arrive dates back to 1620.

Through that ancestry, I have been given word-of-mouth accounts of how forceful The Crown was with regards to how its "subjects" were treated, including how they were permitted to worship their God. How anyone under the rule of the British Crown was stripped of their right to worship, except in The Church established by King Henry VIII: The Church of England. When he banished the Catholic Church from the lands he ruled. Because the Pope dared to deny him the request to divorce his wife, Catherine of Aragon. Due to her failure to "produce a son," the only proper Heir to his kingdom at that time. Henry concluded that no person had more authority than The King. And therefore had no right to tell The

King what he could or could not do. Concerning any matters, including marriage. Henry formed The Church of England and declared The King of the Empire would also act as the Head of the Church: establishing his own clergy. Which is still the practice of England, but now acknowledges a woman's right to inherit The Crown. And control of the Kingdom.

Henry then denounced and forbade any other form of religion or worship as acceptable in his kingdom. Punishable by death if violated.

I have been privileged, thanks to relatives still residing in England, to visit The Martyrs' Memorial positioned at the intersection of St. Giles', Magdalen Street and Beaumont Street to the west of Balliol College, Oxford, England. As well as the beautiful gothic Cathedral where the names of the Martyrs' of the original church grace a wall of the building.

The King also demanded of "his subjects," who were already very heavily taxed, to tithe an additional amount to support his church. Refusing to pay to maintain it from monies collected for the purpose of supporting The Crown. An act which also served to expand the personal wealth of The Crown.

I understand that after enough time had passed, preceding the Revolutionary War, where men of that era somehow managed to defeat the Greatest, Strongest Military of the most Powerful known Empire in the known world at the time. An Empire that, over time, had simply evolved into The United Kingdom of England, became an ally of America. No longer our enemy, the former stronghold we were subjected to. But that should not deter our current government from teaching about the atrocities practiced by The British Empire, in its entirety, atrocities they imposed upon its "subjects." Or teach how, over time, we went from enemy to ally. How they went from the Empire to a United Kingdom, in our public school system. History must be studied. Or it is deemed to repeat itself! As recorded and shown in the Bible.

Those atrocities, like so many other cruel dynasties before them, drove people to seek new lands.

The first amendment drafted by the Founding Fathers into Our Constitution was intended to guarantee to the American citizens that they would never experience what their ancestors experienced during the reign of Henry VIII or all who ruled after him up to King George, who was on the throne when we declared our independence. The most notably voiced concerns, presented to and addressed by Thomas Jefferson. Through back and forth, correspondence with the Bishop and members of The Danbury Baptist Church of Maryland. Letters of correspondence chronicled in what is referred to as The Federalist Papers. Laying to rest that their newly formed federal government was restricted from establishing a preferred religion. The original Pilgrims and Quakers had also fled. Men, women and children bravely willing to risk crossing the Atlantic Ocean. Being met and confronted with only God knew what. If and when they made that crossing, for parts unknown. Where they would at least be free.

Another very important element of that historical period with regards to those brave men and women. The first to arrive and set up roots was the Covenant, already briefly mentioned, along with the name John Carver. The man who helped organize that infamous Mayflower voyage. Many, having studied that voyage, conclude it was Mr. Carver who likely wrote and presented that Covenant to the forty-one adult men before stepping foot off the ship. The Mayflower Compact is also included with The Federalist Papers. Documents gathered and preserved that tell the story of how America came to be.

That first Covenant written begins with, "In the Name of God, Amen. We, whose names are underwritten, the Loyal Subjects of our dread Sovereigne Lord, King James, By the grace of God, of Great Britaine, France, And Ireland, King defender of the Faith, etc. Mr. Carver would go on to be the first Governor of what would become the State of Massachusetts. In the new land, in the Colony they named Plymouth Harbor. That document is short and definitely worth reading. Along with how those brave men women and children began to build their little town. The simple, indisputable fact is that the hearts of the men and women who crossed the Atlantic Ocean to our shores were all focused and centered on God. And willing to rely on Him for their protection.

The purpose of The First amendment was never about keeping religion out of government. It exists to remind all the elected representatives who would precede them they are restricted from ever hindering, dictating or financially demanding the American citizens to support and maintain a government-established church. It was included in Our Constitution to be the ongoing reminder to all that, while in power, they were never to forget: We, The People of the United States, are a self-governing people who have the Right to Worship our God. However, we choose. And that we respect the rights of any fellow citizen who chooses not to acknowledge a God. Or worship any Supreme Deities their ancestors recognize. As well as extending that same respect to anyone who chooses to claim there is no God. It is meant to Specify the freedom of all Religious choices, should never be challenged or questioned. And that religious choices are always to be honored, respected and protected by their elected leaders. Never to forget the Nation they govern was established upon Christian-Judeao values and principles. To be the only nation where all Christians, Jews, Muslims, Hindus, or any other preference, including atheists, could live side by side in peace and harmony. Out of mutual respect for one another. It was never intended to be used to challenge, restrict or deny the rights of any American citizen. Or worse yet, to try and pit one group of citizens against another based on religious beliefs, as many are demanding in today's culture!

Now you know!

The study of history fascinates me. All history. And has brought me to the conclusion the rise and fall of every civilization, every great empire, every society and culture has been in some way connected to their belief systems. Or lack thereof. Something drives them to power, and something ultimately causes their demise. There's a book in the bible meant to explain that very process. It's called Ecclesiastes. Where it proclaims, "there is nothing new under the sun."

Ultimately, I believe we began our demise when we accepted the Engel vs. Vitale federal court rendered ruling, as an acceptable nationwide practice. It was the first step we, as a people, a culture, and a society, took that led to the slow continued relinquishing of our freedoms back to a ruling entity. Where in America, it was never meant to be. It was always designed to remain with the people. It was when we were coerced into accepting and placing man's ways above God's ways. It was when we began trying to please people instead of God. When we began doing what mankind told us to do instead of what God demands of us in order to receive his blessings and protection! Thank God through His mercy, He ignored that decision when the Supreme Court decided it wasn't essential or fundamental to let children acknowledge God or His presence! Continuing to uphold the Covenant that had been presented to Him: First by Mr. John Carver and then reiterated when those fifty six men presented it to Him a second time. When they severed all ties from The King of the British Empire and acknowledged God as The

One True King of America for all peoples of all nationalities. For all times! Let's explore a different approach that could have been taken. One considering all parties involved. Current along with all future generations of America. People who disagreed with that verdict should have demanded our elected officials correct this dual violation of our right to worship. Our right to free speech, which includes speaking about our belief in God. Stopping the third branch of the government from thinking they could determine where or how we could participate in free speech.

By permitting them to think, they could tell us where we could speak of, to, or and about our God. We should have demanded that the congressional body, at the time, challenge the courts' intent to impose law from the bench instead of in the halls of congress. Where we agreed and accepted, it could be considered. That was when we began surrendering to following rules placed upon us by people we had not elected to represent us over an element of our lives. In the case of Engel vs. Vitale: The Most essential element of our lives. We should have demanded our elected representatives to uphold and protect our Constitution. Which they all take an oath to protect when entering office. Which is there to protect us and our rights as a free people! But since we neglected to do just that, it became very easy for career politicians or governing bodies to use the court system to unconstitutionally push an anti-god, anti-constitutional agenda upon the citizens of America. Noting a large majority of citizens seemed to silently accept the opinion of those seven unelected men wearing robes of justice. Men who, in that Case decision, tipped the scales of justice in our nation against God. In favor of a Humanistic, Communistic approach, where no mention of God is tolerated or accepted. We missed what the Bible explained as God's view on silence. When you remain silent you are expressing approval! In the eyes of the federal government, they, too, read silence to mean we are approving of what they are doing. Now, looking back over the decades, if we are willing to look at the reality, we see how politicians have chosen to use our silence as a tool to establish a secular, non-religious nation. For them, Problem's solved; when it comes to the hot topic, moral issues they deem too touchy to tackle. Seen as threatening issues that could be used to remove them from power.

In their eyes they were free to change what is truly a moral issue into a political issue. Knowing since they were never challenged over not addressing the Engel vs. Vitale decision, it's how they chose to handle all the moral issues that present themselves. Instead of addressing them head-on, they can let them take their good old time working its way through the lengthy, drawn-out legal system. Or, if beneficial to enhance a re-election, use it as a campaign issue they'll never address. So, like Pilate either way, they can wash their hands of what they decreed, too politically charged to push back against. And just let the mob have what they want. This was the beginning of The Silent Majority. What has led us, I believe, into a situation very similar to what is written at the end of the Book of

Judges as recorded in the Hebrew Bible 21:25: "In those days there was no King in Israel. All people did what was right in their own eyes."

I can only speak for myself, but when I look at what is happening here in America, that's a spot-on description of what is taking place on our soil. No recognition of Our true King. And not enough leaders to uphold our founding principles, Recognizing who that King is and His role in the stability of our nation. Everyone seems to be doing what is right in their eyes, living their own so-called truth.

Abraham Lincoln was the last president willing to face head-on, the great moral issue. One that affected not only our nation but all of mankind during his place in America's history of slavery. He forewarned us….

"America will never be destroyed from the Outside. If we falter and lose our freedoms, it will be because we destroyed Ourselves." Folks, I think enough of us realize that is exactly what has been happening since 1962.

Starting with a few very bad judges. Rendering bad decisions with regards to God's place in our nation. And our society. And if, like me, you view the world through a biblical lens, you can't help but see God's enemy behind it all. The one, according to the Bible, who comes to lie, cheat and destroy. Devouring everything in its path. Lies upon lies upon lies. One empty promise after another. One twisted, distorted version of the truth after another. And the continued altering of the true meaning of words. Coupled with the intentional creation of different words designed to alter God's reality. And subvert the truth. In the case of Engel vs Vitale, a couple who did not identify as American but as Communists residing in America. Clinging to their communistic viewpoint with regards to God. A viewpoint The exact opposite of America's founding principles. Communists who were determined to instill that viewpoint onto the American soil. In an effort to change the American way of thinking. And our very way of life. They were not residing here as friends, my friends. They were transplanted here by God's enemy! Along with over a million refugees from war-torn European countries. Sadly, many of those granted asylum in our country began the process of forcing God out of America. America has always been a welcoming nation. Sadly, their goal was to alter America. Not assimilate to our ways. Something which is still going on to this very day!

Engel vs. Vitale was the first case against God that made its way to the Supreme Court of America. But not the last. It happened three more times during the Nineteen Seventies. Major Cases, in nature, that continued to push us further away from our God honoring values leading to a more secular form of society. Becoming intolerant of God and those who believe in Him. And His ways of life.

One such case of which would become a stain upon our nation that trickled beyond our shores around the globe. A blood-red stain much darker in color than slavery. January of 1973. We'll argue that case later! But let's get back to addressing the point of abiding by the rule of the court instead of through properly drafted and approved legislation. Because according to our Constitution, only our elected congress members, beholden to us, their electorate, have been authorized by us, the governed body, to propose legislation. For our consideration and approval. And the fact that only then can it become an acceptable law of the land.

All taking place only after a grueling debate among all members of both houses. Followed by a vote that must be approved by a simple majority. First in the lower house then the senate. If no suggested amendments are proposed from the Senate floor, it goes to the president. If amendments make it into the bill by a simple majority of the Senate, it must be presented back to the congress for acceptance of proposed amendments. Now, if a president vetoes proposed legislation, it is returned to the joint houses, and if it meets with a two-thirds majority vote, it is sent back to the president, who is required to accept the will of the people and sign it into law. Whether he agrees or not!

This is the strenuous, arduous process our Founding Fathers placed upon those elected to the governmental body. Intended to make it extremely difficult and thought-provoking to even attempt to impose restrictions upon free people! Not even the highest elected office in our nation, the office of the presidency has the authority to go against the will and desires of the people. Amazing set of checks and balances! No wonder it took so long to fine-tune. The third equal separate branch, our Judicial Branch, was established to uphold our Constitution, and only laws properly self-imposed and in agreement with the will of the people, for the safety of people. Their purpose and their powers are defined in the three sections of Article III of The Constitution. And nowhere within those articles were they granted the authority to impose a ruling on the electorate, let alone dictate from the bench a preferred lifestyle. Their decisions are to be rendered based on constitutionally drafted legislation that has been signed into law. And to uphold the rights of the free people as outlined in Our Constitution and Bill of Rights. Our Founding Fathers put into place three separate, equally important branches of government to keep check on one another. A simply brilliant concept never before imagined. Try to convince me they weren't listening to the whispers and taking direction from God during that lengthy moment in time! It has been noted during more than one deadlock during the first convention of states, Benjamin Franklin suggested to stop debating an issue of contention and pray upon it before picking it up again.

That said, in my humble opinion, the issue of Engel vs Vitale never should have been accepted by the court for consideration. It was not within the court's responsibility to the people! To rehash a settled matter from the Convention of Delegates that established Our

Constitution. Because a couple disagreed with The most important principles of our country. Open expression of Religion through protected free speech. The Engels demanded the complete denial of the rights of every American citizen, regarding religion and speech, to accommodate their belief system. Something unthinkable, let alone unheard of, in any nation under communist rule! The issue of not wanting their son exposed to the mere idea of God could have been resolved very easily by suggesting the plaintiff send their son to school after the prayer had been recited. Instead, members of that judicial body had no problem stripping away and violating the freedoms of every child to ever enter our public school system. Also, ignoring the opinions of every parent, other than the Engle's. Parents and citizens whose local taxes support those public schools, I might add. Sixty years worth of American citizens' freedoms have been trampled on by those six men since that day. While at the same time, for the past sixty years, the individual states have been forced to conform all curricula around an unconstitutionally ruled federal format. Instead of how their residents, who foot the bills, prefer it to be done!

That is how we got from there to where we are today. Again, tolerating one such court ruling after another. Combined with some very bad legislation also left unchallenged. And the gridlock brought about by career politicians ignoring the voice of the people who are willing to speak up. Simply demanding what they are entitled to under our Constitution! Also guaranteed in the First Amendment.

"To petition the government for a redress of grievances." Evan Esar quotes quite accurately, "Many a politician who's been appointed acts as if he's been anointed."

The Supreme Court's ruling on the Engel vs. Vitale case, as I've mentioned, was only the first of many, beginning in the early Sixties, that really changed our country. Began to shift the mindset and way of thinking of many. Conflicting opinions with regards to heavy United States Military involvement in The Vietnam War also sharply impacted, causing great division among the military-aged generation of the time. Including people in politics and those contemplating entering the "political area" for the sole purpose of changing what they disagreed with. What they did not like or approve of, with regards to the morals and value standards of America that clashed with theirs. The way things were viewed also shifted. From holding fast to our founding principles. To a nuanced belief, it no longer was necessary to convince a simple majority of the elected to agree with oneself. Having witnessed, for decades now, that with the right lawyers and the right judge, and at least one irate individual or group, one elected person could accomplish anything the majority would never agree upon. And issues that fell in the category of moral issues could be a constant cause for reelection. Never meant to be resolved. Always the necessary tool in their political toolbox! I know I am not the only American citizen who realizes our government stopped operating as it was intended decades ago. No longer being a representative body upholding the best interests, freedoms, and God-given rights of all its citizens. Intended with the most minimal amount of interference in how we choose to live our lives. Our government has become filled with autocrats and career politicians choosings to serve those who help feed their addiction to power. And keep them in Office. Using the very heavy hand of the numerous alphabet agencies, they established along the way to once again impose their preferred way of living onto the American citizens. Through unconstitutional regulations not only on the Citizens but also through Corporate America. Instilling their opinions on how they are permitted to operate here in America!

Those Supreme Court rulings are in and of themselves a direct violation of Our Constitution. Nowhere in the Constitution does it state or grant the Judicial branch jurisdiction on how American citizens are to live. That authority lies solely with the people. Not on their interpretation. Not what the majority of the justices want it to be. Their reason for existence within our government is to determine if what the other two branches do are clearly in agreement with the powers awarded to them by The Constitution. Is a charge against a citizen just? Is a protected right of a citizen being violated? And on rare occasions, to determine if a previous court overstepped its authority. Our judicial branch is charged to consider and render a decision on all of those things. But they are NOT permitted to MAKE laws. That is not included in their specifically listed duties and responsibilities to the American citizens. Their primary objective is to make sure the government doesn't overstep its authority. And impose unconstitutional restrictions upon the people. That those elected represent and protect our rights and freedoms at all times; and to ensure what they do is never in conflict with those protected rights. Which is beginning to happen. Thank God! Newly presented cases are challenging the validity of the rulings of those cases from the Sixties and Seventies.

The very first article of our constitution states, "All legislative Powers herein granted shall be vested in a Congress of the United States, which shall consist of a Senate and House of Representative." All of which are elected by the people to be their voice within the body of the government. This is the absolute beauty that defines the United States of America. We, The People, have the final say. Having been given a voice in our government. For the first time in the history of mankind. Our voices are to be heard and honored by those we entrust to represent us in our government. This is why The Constitution of the United States is considered The Most Unique Document ever written! The reason is worth repeating. The checks and balances put in place by our Founding Fathers, with the utmost thought-through manner, to ensure the voice of the people always has the final say. Sadly most of us know that is not the case of how the current federal government, in this pivotal time in our history, views things. Half of the electorate is completely ignored. Other than to be shamed. Ridiculed. Degraded. And accused of being a threat to our democracy. At least according to the democrats and members of the establishment. That has managed to stay in the Halls of our federal government far too long.

A huge faction of one political party, along with established politicians desperate to remain in power, are dead set on having the 26 states who do not agree with their agenda fall in line. And surrender to their opinion on how the nation should function. Again a direct violation of the individual rights of each state. Totally and completely indifferent and uncaring to the rights or reasons of why people decide where they choose to live within the boundaries of our Country. Which, in turn, determines the direct needs of that particular area of our nation. I offer a few examples. The needs of our predominantly farm or ranch areas are completely different from the states with major cities. Although each state has at least one major city. While another example is how some states flourish from having predominantly major cities, coupled with farmlands scattered about or our National Parks, feeding a lucrative tourist element of their economy. While others share space to satisfy the industrial, or manufacturing needs of our nation. And yet others that abound in the natural much needed resources that supply our energy requirements. Another unique quality about The United States. Each individual State has the authority to govern in the manner that best fulfills the needs of the residents.

The entire concept behind establishing a Self-Governing nation the first in the history of the modern world. And only the second attempt in the recorded history of mankind, for those of you who were not taught that very important fact, was grounded in The belief we all answer to a Higher Power. A Creator. Our Founding Fathers went to the only Real Documented reference of a race of people longing to try. When those brave men took on the task of convincing thirteen colonies to forfeit their dependence on The King of the British Empire for their survival and attempt to induce enough confidence in them to form a nation of free people. Already having proven to themselves, they were able to use their God-given free will, stamina, determination and abilities to survive without a king. Since they'd been successful at it for more than one hundred years. Certain that placing their trust in their God, The Ultimate King, they were sure to succeed! Those men poured over the Bible, with heavy concentration on Deuteronomy, the words of instruction God gave to Moses to help His people.

Following their exodus from Egypt. Keenly aware that after generations in bondage and slavery at the hands of the Egyptian Pharaoh, they needed instructions on how to live and become self-sufficient again. That if they were willing to surrender to His will and live explicitly as He told them, they could be a free people. With no need for any other ruler to tell them what to do. All of this was in exchange for their freedom. He laid before them the blessings and the curse and called the heavens and the earth as His witnesses. Sadly, many of the older generation that had fled Egypt had become too set in their ways. Unable to cope and adapt to the hardships of the desert, and began to complain. It was a hard, grueling existence in Egypt, but at least they knew what to expect. Some went so far as to demand Moses take them back lest they die in the desert. The rest of the story gets even more interesting! Due to their own lack of trust in the One who rescued them, the oldest generation never got to enter the promised land.

Among the dozen sent to scout out the land, only two were confident that with God's help, they could, in fact, overtake the land from those already there. Only those two were rewarded entrance into The Land of Milk and Honey as they described what they had seen to the elders upon their return to camp! The rest weren't strong enough in their faith. Had been unwilling to remain focused on their God. Quickly forgetting the wonders He had performed right before their very eyes. They became stuck and condemned to die in the wilderness; they'd been subjected to wander for forty years. Due to their verbal lack of faith and trust. Are too many Americans also losing their focus and misplacing their trust in our elected leaders? Leaders who have been failing them for more than forty years now. Are we getting complacent? Willing to hand over our freedom in exchange for the basics. Longing to be left alone, content with nothing more? Forty years of aimless wandering, interesting. Coincidence? Are we really willing to settle? No longer wanting to pursue. Are we relinquishing our rights to the people who continue pouring into our country illegally, bending to the different sets of values they are bringing into our country?

Again, as before people with no intention to assimilate to the American Way of Life. People who openly demonstrate against our values. Impulsed by our lifestyle. People who are persistent in thinking they have the right to take our country from us and make it their own. Millions of whom see nothing wrong with breaking our laws to enter. And elected politicians who have no interest in stopping the invasion. People who worship a different god or in a different manner than ourselves? Which they have the right to do, as do we. But are we going to continue to yield to their demands who chose not to believe in any Higher power? Are we going to surrender and live as an exiled people within our own country? Since there are no new lands to conquer. I hope not! And I believe millions of Americans feel exactly the same way. Like me, millions of other citizens see a person, questionably elected, obviously not mentally stable enough, to the office of the presidency. A person who goes from fits of anger to times of total age-related confusion. A person acting more like an anointed ruler than a person elected to represent the best interests of the American Citizens.

And our great Nation. A person who pledged to strive for unity if elected to consider what is best for all the American citizens! Not just those who cast a vote in favor of what he said he would do. Or for his political affiliation. Although, I must say Mr. Biden never really said he intended to do the excessive progressive things he's doing. Make the radical changes he's making. Never explaining this was, in fact, his intent if he was elected. He promised to unite the people. None of these drastic changes in both foreign and domestic policy were presented to the American people for their approval during his isolated campaign. He just promised to put an end to [the media-induced] chaos surrounding the Trump Presidency. Chaos all stirred up by the democrats who verbally and violently opposed his election.

Mr. Biden also managed to deceive millions of Americans trapped in a media-induced fear of dying if they were infected with the COVID-19 virus. Pretentiously factually announcing he knew how to "crush it." Which, in my humble opinion, is brazenly proclaiming to have more power than God. While President Trump tried to deal with reality. Sadly, but truthfully, conceding to the fact "it wasn't going away, we have to learn how to live with it." It's still here, folks! Just like the Hong Kong flu that hit our shores in September of 1968 and still raises its ugly head every year, now dubbed as the flu season. Who spoke the truth? Who proclaimed to be able to do what only God could do? Only you know who you choose to believe and why. I hope you've thought them through. If not, please do so before you cast a vote in November of 2024. Please remember who swore they would never impose a mandatory vaccine but did. Who forced our youngest children to participate in a national drug experiment. That has proven to be very harmful in a variety of ways. Who tried to say the broken supply chain issue was only temporary yet is still haunting us with empty shelves and excessive lengthy wait times for materials of all types. Including

Medical Supplies. Who denied our children a proper education? Who is introducing pornographic poison to our very youngest, most vulnerable children? Who is openly subjecting our children to sterilization through surgical mutilation? The same one who is demanding we surrender our will and our core beliefs to the government. To him and his line of thinking. Despite what we believe about serving and obeying Our God.

These policies Mr. Biden is imposing, mostly by executive fiat. Because he and the members of the democratic party know they would never be accepted and approved through the legislative procedure. Policies that are, in fact, imposing extremely challenging financial hardships on millions upon millions of Americans. But most notably impacting the middle class and those already trapped in perpetual poverty, I refer to it as the democratic owned and controlled by plantation. The way I see things, the democratic party had to concede to the North with regards to slavery. But they have never stopped fighting to control our country. By taking total control of our federal government. Most of us know of at least one person, one family, one neighbor, one relative, truly struggling to stay afloat. Especially families with children. If not, you are one of those people C.S. Lewis was referring to when he said, "One of the most cowardly things ordinary people do is to shut their eyes to facts." And I implore you to look into your heart when something offends you. Because it will fall on one side or the other of what God approves of!

But I am certain God will bless those families making the necessary sacrifices for their innocent children. Children, I might add, who are going to be handed the bills that they will have to pass on to their children from the out-of-control spending of this administration. Passed on through heavy taxation. Seems to me like we're heading right back where we started when we became known as The Great American experiment! We, as a people, must realize we have the ability of declaring our independence once again. This time from the establishment, our federal government has evolved over the last Seventy years! Actually, we did just that in the 2016 election. And they have been in revolt ever since! How dare we send an outsider into their exclusive club!

One they'd thought they'd successfully made impenetrable from the outside world. Just take a moment to think about their behavior since we, the people, refused to accept the potential candidates that met with their approval back in 2015. And against all odds, succeeded in getting Donald Trump elected. Something they couldn't fathom would actually happen. Considered an absolute joke. After all, it was Hillary Rodham Clinton's turn. Those so strongly in opposition to President Trump are still in temper tantrum mode! Determined, he along with his family, must be destroyed in every way on every level! What did Donald J. Trump ever do that makes him so despised and hated by the ruling class? The fact that he actually kept his campaign promises. Could The fact that he did not need the approval of the establishment or the money of the establishment, which means he can't be bought or controlled by the establishment, have anything to do with this disdain? After all, until Mr. Trump entered the political area, he was one of the one percent referred to as The Elites. Do they feel threatened because he sides with the average American Citizen instead of them?

The very idea of declaring our independence from the most powerful Kingdom in the world at the time took an act of bravery most of us could never begin to comprehend. After all, the only Military was the British Imperial Army. The colonies had no army. They formed a Militia. Willing to take on that Giant. And far too many Americans fail to seek out the facts or appreciate or know enough about our historical founding. Starting with the simple fact that those fifty-six men clearly understood, signing their names on that Document, declaring to the known world that they refused to be subjected to the tyranny of King George any longer, was no different than signing their own execution order. They were, after all, committing the ultimate act of treason in the eyes of The King. They were revolting against the mightiest army in the world. They understood the severity of their actions. And did it anyway! Not for themselves but for the sake of the people living in the thirteen colonies, who could no longer tolerate the cruelty of how they were being treated. Taxation without representation is only one of the many grievances they deemed they could no longer endure.

I share with you the closing sentence from Our Declaration of Independence. "And for the support of this Declaration, with the firm Reliance on the Protection of Divine Providence, we mutually pledge to each other our Lives, our Fortunes, and our sacred honor." If you haven't read The Declaration of Independence in a while, do yourself a favor. Actually, the Declaration of Independence, along with The Constitution, should be considered as a two-part form of study. You would think it was written to be presented to the current federal government as you read the list of grievances against the King noted. The very reasons why they were stating, in writing, for the known world to see, they'd had enough! And were willing to fight and die for what they believed was right.

Here is a single paragraph to give you an idea of what happened to most of them. Five were captured, declared traitors by the Crown and brutally tortured. Nine of them fought in the Revolutionary war and died from wounds or hardships. Two lost their sons to the war. Two others had sons captured by the British. And at least a dozen had their homes pillaged and burned by the British army. A far cry from the myth of being a bunch of rich, privileged old white men! For the record, the average age was forty-four with more than a dozen thirty-five or younger, the youngest being Thomas Lynch Jr., twenty-seven from the colony of South Carolina. Also, for the record, not all of those fifty-six men were of Anglo-Saxon origin.

It is believed that a mere two million people lived in the thirteen colonies at the time. A number that became divided into three factions. The Patriots, those willing to fight The Loyalists, and those who thought it safer to remain loyal to the Crown, and those who longed to stay Neutral. But in the end, nine of the thirteen colonies were convinced and voted in favor of The Declaration. Knowing they were destined to be met with military resistance and possibly years of hardship. But in the end, their desire for freedom far outweighed, remaining under the rulership of The tyrannical King, won out.

Many, I believe, have at least heard of the infamous statement Patrick Henry [from Virginia] used in the speech he delivered to the Second Virginia Convention of March 23rd, 1775, when he so boldly proclaimed, "Give me liberty or give me death!" In his endeavor to encourage and mobilize the residents of Virginia to join in taking action against the British Rule over the Colonies, stressing that achieving peace by submitting to British rule would never be possible in any circumstance.

Thank God enough of them were determined and willing to risk their lives. Women were willing to sacrifice fathers, husbands, sons, male friends, and extended family members, all because they embraced those words in the opening sentence of the second paragraph of The Declaration of Independence. Words that rang true that had been presented to them for their consideration. "We hold these truths to be self-evident, that all men are created equal, that they are endowed by their Creator with certain unalienable Rights, that among these are Life, Liberty, and the Pursuit of Happiness - That to secure these Rights, Governments are instituted among Men, deriving their Powers from the Consent of the Governed, that whenever any Form of Government becomes destructive of These

Ends, it is The Right of The People to alter or abolish it, and to institute new Government, laying its Foundation on such Principles, and organizing its Powers in such a Form, as to them shall seem most likely to effect Safety and Happiness."

Never in the history of mankind had any society declared such a powerful proclamation against a Ruling Empire. That no other man or woman [King or Queen] had the right to proclaim a higher status over another. Or had the authority to impose a class of status onto a person. With the intention of clearly implying they were beneath them. And it was where they were destined to remain. Moses needed to plead with the Pharaoh of Egypt to let the people, who would become known as Hebrews, free! With a whole lot of persuasive help from God ...

For those of you who were not taught this fact until the founding of the United States of America, there were Rulers and subjects. America gave birth to the very concept of shared citizenship among all people. And with that, presented the second greatest gift offered to humanity. The freedom to accomplish whatever one was willing to strive to achieve. The right and ability to dream big dreams. And make them a reality. Most notably the rise of what is referred to as The Middle Class Citizen. In all other cultures, there were the Rich, who ruled. Those beholden to the Rich, who controlled every element of their lives, and were fully aware that one slip and they became like everyone else. The poor are also beholden to the rich for their very survival. I note here, The Greatest Gift ever offered was the gift of Salvation. Through the suffering, death and resurrection of The Son of God! But what America gave to all of mankind is a fabulous second! Freedom.

Before moving on, I will state the obvious: the delegates from the original 13 Colonies failed miserably at addressing and being able to remedy slavery. Unable to come up with any acceptable solution to those primarily from the southernmost colonies. Where the largest number of people owned slaves. I think it's worth mentioning, however, that there were some very prominent influential people of color in a few of the major cities, including Philadelphia, at the time, who had a few slaves. Mostly house slaves, but slaves all the same. Also worthy of mention among the group of men forever known as The Founding Fathers is James Forten [1766-1842] of Philadelphia. Born a free person of African American descent. A sailmaker by profession. Who set sail to fight for our independence in 1781. Another fact is that despite efforts to make it seem like most of the Colonists, and especially those fifty-six men, owned slaves, only twelve American Presidents did, in fact, own slaves before it was abolished here in America. Slavery was not resolved before the actual Signing of the Declaration of Independence. But again, thanks be to God, it remained a front-and-center issue until it reached the boiling point and turned into a war that threatened to tear our union apart. Again, for those of you who were not taught this fact, The Free people of the United States of America were the first in the world to denounce and reject slavery, to the point of waging war against each other to end it. Up until that time, owning slaves had been common practice. It's also recorded all throughout the recorded history of the Jewish people in the Torah and the Bible. From 1858 until the election of President Abraham Lincoln, The House was severely Divided over the issue of slavery. Upon his election, President Lincoln, the first candidate to represent the newly formed Republican Political Party, drafted The Emancipation Proclamation, Enacted and signed into law on January 1, 1863. The Document demanding anyone in The United States who owned slaves set them free. Making it perfectly clear that any State or partial state not complying, would be deemed in rebellion of The United States. Before that famous proclamation, Rulers, Kings and Aristocrats gave themselves the right to own slaves. Just as the Rulers and kings of Africa gave themselves the rights to sell their own people into slavery. Because there was no one brave enough to challenge their self-imposed authority. And sadly, far too often, the common person, lacking the means to satisfy a debt, had no recourse but to surrender themselves or a member of the family into slavery as payment of a debt.

This is what the establishment of America radically changed. Not just benefiting the American citizens but people from other nations who followed suit. We were the Shining City on a hill meant to be an example to the world. We were a people who understood the difference between right and wrong in the eyes of God and embraced doing the right thing! Willing to die to secure the rights of others. "In order to form a more perfect union." Accepting the fact our human limitations made it impossible to reach perfection. But that was no excuse or reason to never stop us from striving towards perfection. Driven by always at least attempting to do the right thing.

As I have pointed out, we began down this road of self-destruction decades ago. And there are people currently in our federal government responsible for steering us down this path of collapse. People always promising if we just re-elect them to one more term in office. If we just understand the additional taxes and, fees and regulations they are imposing, are all necessary to ensure they finally have what it takes to fix things. To be able to create that Great Society, Johson said, was attainable.

My friends, these people are the problem. They created the problems, struggles, challenges and hardships plaquing the people of our nation. And the longer they have been able to remain in power, the more difficult, self-serving and arrogant they've become. Openly refusing to follow and abide by the very limitations imposed upon them by Our Constitution. They are a class of people desperate, hell-bent and determined to be able to tell us what rights and freedoms we can have. Not to mention the fact that they are taking the wages of at least three out of the five days we work each week to support ourselves and our families. Is it any wonder millions of the average American find it necessary to have a part-time job because the full-time paycheck isn't enough anymore?! Is it any wonder why young couples think long and hard and struggle over whether or not they can afford to bring the child they long for into this world. All due to the reckless inconsiderate spending on behalf of our elected. From our individual counties, cities, states and federal government, every branch wants a portion of what we make, leaving us just barely enough to survive. We really do work for them, not for ourselves. My friends, we are right back to where we started. Beholding to those in leadership. People who have somehow acquired generational wealth while supposedly representing the People. I know how Donald Trump made his money. Built an empire. He took a relatively modest inheritance his father made in the real estate market in New York and turned it into a global enterprise. One, I might add that, offers jobs to every element of the average middle-class person. Just about every step on the ladder of the middle class is given opportunities in and through The Trump Organization. From the Architect to the Chambermaid to the Golf Catty and every job or position in between. Can't say the same for any of the people in Washington, DC. Other than the millions they employ on our tax dollars through the continued expansion of our government. Pretty safe to say they are the people who keep them in office. To insure their very generous salaries, benefits and pensions. All at our expense! Our very government has become our Landlord! Leaving us barely enough to survive; just like so many of our ancestors who'd been willing to brave the unknown to escape the cruelty and greed of their landlords. Here are just a few hard, eye-opening facts to ponder. According to Zillow, to own a home now in the year 2024 requires an income of $106,000. Yet just a mere four years ago, with $59,000 yearly, the American citizen could purchase an average home. Now for the harsh reality, currently the median household income in America is $75,000. A whopping 41% below the income necessary to own a home. In other words, right now there is no way to achieve the American Dream for those entering adulthood. Something must be done to correct that injustice. The difference between our ancestors and us is we have no more new frontiers. No unknown worlds to escape to. Which calls to mind, at least for me, a line from a song written by Don Henley and Glenn Frey of The Eagles, it's titled The Last Resort. A song about the settling of California. Our last frontier reminds the listener that there's nowhere else to go ... "We've got to make it here!"

I worked in the restaurant industry for years. And it was a pretty well known fact as soon as one or two employees got fired. The owners decided some of their employees were losing sight of who the boss was, getting a little too comfortable.... and started letting people who'd been there any length of time go. They were "cleaning house." And if you were in the industry any time at all, you knew it was better to look for another restaurant or diner that was hiring rather than wait for the hatchet to drop. Folks, it's long past time, We The People started cleaning out the house! Our House. Because these career politicians have been there so long, they no longer see it as The People's House. It's become the house meant to serve their interests and the interests of those who keep funding their campaigns. Getting them reelected. It's become all about cutting deals. I think of how they operate in terms of running a high-stakes poker game using The People's House to set up those games. Someone had to sponsor them, front them financially, to even get them into the game. And someone else needed to front them more money to sit at one of the tables. And they kept needing to find others willing to give them more money to stay in the game. Especially if they longed to go to the big-money games in the private back rooms, where the real action took place. Where the real deals were negotiated and cut. Because most of them only ever won something about once every two years. But believed if they could just borrow enough money to stay at it through one more election cycle, eventually they'd hit big. How exhaustive and addictive. What a way to live.

They've gotten too beholden to their bankers to get out! Too addicted to playing the game. They can't give it up. Don't believe me, some of them have been in the game for more than forty years! And they are completely out of touch with We the People. And worst yet, many of them don't seem to care that we've actually figured it out. They really believe they are untouchable.

The current administration of our federal government, along with a few key Democrat-controlled states, have declared war against more than half of the Voting Block of America. Last count, at least seventy-five million. And once again the people are divided into three factions. People who have been deceived, who support and are pushing for these radical changes. People who strongly oppose these radical changes. And those who have stayed neutral, hoping, longing and praying for things to go back to their preconceived notion of normal. A time when they didn't have to engage. Where they could remain the safe, silent majority. Who went along to get along and remain blissfully unnoticed. Sound familiar? Because it is, it's happened all throughout history.

Only you know where you stand! Whether you serve God or man. Whether you aim to please God. Or the government. Or yourself! Are you a person willing to be obedient to God or the government? Sadly, far too many chose government over God during the covid virus lockdowns. Agreeing when the government declared attending church services were non-essential. But accepted them, saying Liquor Stores, Marijuana dispensaries were. When we bowed to letting our relatives die alone with no formal burial. Tolerating abortion clinics having no regulations; while most surgical procedures were put on hold. If not considered life-threatening.

The current president is on record saying ... "I ran for president because I believed we were in a battle for the soul of our nation." Powerful words. Great speech writer. Something he repeats often. But If you believe in God, if you have any knowledge of God's teachings in The Bible, or the Torah, there is only one way to view that statement. When you look at the laws Mr. Biden is enforcing on the American citizen, it is very clear he is truly NOT on the side of God! Who was, for a very long time, the Soul of our nation. Mr.

Biden not only demands we "render unto Caesar what belongs to Caesar," he is demanding we surrender unto him what belongs to God. He is insistent we abandon God's commands and honor his wishes and desires instead. All of which are evil. He's not the only person in our federal government proclaiming to be a Catholic. But is one of many who obviously have no inkling on what it means or how to live a Christian life. I'm not alone when I say these so-called Catholics are Cino's catholic in name only, which doesn't fare well in the eyes of God.

I choose to stand with God. I choose to obey God. And much rather prefer to place my trust in God than the government. Especially one that has an exceptionally bad track record. And seems out and out determined to break the Covenant our Founding Fathers formed with God. I thank God He honors the desire of those in our nation who still ask Him to uphold it for His Glory and those who love and obey Him.

I am willing to fight. Engage. And I know I'm not alone. But don't think for a minute it's going to be easy. Can't undo fifty some years of damage overnight. The famous quote, "Power tends to corrupt, and absolute power corrupts absolutely," in my humble opinion, is a fair and accurate description of where our federal government stands today. Absolutely corrupt. It has become its own Beast. One that has grown many tentacles, and its sole purpose has become its own survival. Nothing else matters. NOTHING!

So, where do we go from here? And is it possible to slay The Beast?

Let's start with remembering what David said when he faced Goliath, "You come against me with sword and spear and javelin, but I come against you in the name of the LORD Almighty, the God of the armies of Israel, whom you have defied. This day, the Lord will hand you over to me, and I'll strike you down and cut off your head."

Psalm 118:8 tells us, "It is better to take refuge in the Lord than to trust in man."

Were you one of the people who chose to put your trust in Joe Biden? Without really looking into what he has actually accomplished during his 40-plus-year career in Washington DC. Other than accumulating generational wealth? Did you cast a vote against President Trump because the media convinced you he is evil? A true enemy of our country.

Food for thought! George Washington was Enemy Number One as far as King George was concerned. Abraham Lincoln was The Enemy of The South. And Donald Trump is considered enemy number one of The Establishment. The Entity that feeds and protects THE BEAST!

So, can America be saved? Can the Beast be defeated?

Those questions can only be answered one way... Yes! But NOT WITHOUT GOD!

But we must realize God didn't make this mess. We allowed it to happen. God didn't cause this chaos. He is the God of Order. God did not abandon America. But millions of Americans choose to abandon God. Including many people God permitted to rise to positions of power. Who, instead of listening to Him, fearing Him, started acting like they were a god. Simply put, they forgot they will answer to Him the instant they draw their last breath. It is written in Luke 12:48: "From everyone who has been given much, much will be demanded: and from the one who has been entrusted with much, much more will be asked." I think there's a lot of people in powerful positions in deep trouble with God! People who stopped doing what they took an Oath to do. Elected officials and leaders who began yielding to the enormous temptations that come with power. Starting with massive doses of ego and pride. And a whole lot of greed. Then without even realizing it, they began serving THE BEAST they created.

When I think of some of the people who have been in Washington, DC., for decades now, my thoughts immediately go to Luke's account of how Satan tempted Jesus while He was in the desert. I think it's important to state he didn't tempt him immediately. According to Luke's account, he waited forty days, during which time Jesus had been fasting and, I am certain, had been praying and communing with God heavily centered on what he was about to embark upon. The mission of saving mankind. Beginning with His ministry which would ultimately end, taking him to the Cross.

Luke writes that when those forty days were over, Jesus was hungry, and I can only imagine weighted down by the heavy burden He had willingly chosen to take upon himself, [for our sake] that was when the devil appeared. And after a failed attempt at his human need for food, he took him up and showed him all of the Kingdoms of the world in a single instant and said to him, "I shall give to you all this power and glory; for it has been handed over to me, and I may give it to whomever I wish. And all of this will be yours, if you worship me." Jesus replied, "It is written: You shall worship the Lord, your God, and Him alone shall you serve." And later in his ministry, Jesus forewarned, in Mark 8 verse 36, "For what shall it profit a man, if he shall gain the whole world, and lose his own soul?"

It is painfully clear, by their actions, at least to me, that many of these people aren't even aware of the fact that somewhere during their time in power, they began worshiping Satan. By compromising one truth. Then, one ounce of morality. Followed by a willingness to bend one rule. Stretch one truth. Change the meaning of one word. Until finally, they were serving the evil one instead of God. And worse yet, they have definitely begun to mock God. Put God to the test. By challenging everything that God deems as good. Upholding it with evil. Insisting that what is offensive in the eyes of God must be considered acceptable behavior. And if not embraced, you are obviously a bigot. Or the newly penned phrase, "a Christian nationalist." Or a "dangerous traditional catholic." And if we disagree and refuse to go along, they've come up with lots of names besides a bigot, intended to insult, shame, and intimidate us into silence. And at the present time, maybe for the first time since The Civil War, we have political prisoners being held in federal prisons. For being accused of committing a misdemeanor offense, you can be subject to time in a federal prison. Solely because they were brave enough to show up in massive numbers to challenge them. Another guaranteed right in our First Amendment. Petition to redress grievances…..

However, with regards to the name calling [or labeling] or attempts at shaming or intimidating, I'm going to stay with the old-fashioned claim of my childhood years, "sticks and stones can break my bones, but names can never hurt me." Thank God! And I will hold tight to what my Lord and Savior advised me when I chose to follow him, "Blessed are you when people insult you, persecute you and falsely say all kinds of evil against you because of me. Rejoice and be glad because great is your reward in heaven…" Mathew 5:11. Then, In John 15:18, we were told by Jesus, "If the world hates you, know that it has hated me before it hated you."

And speaking of God, let's take a look at a few more statements He has made. First, with regards to the final instructions He gave to the Jews [after wandering aimlessly for forty years, I might add] right before they crossed the Jordan River into the Promised Land...

of which there are a few variations depending on word translation [the Bible I am using Quest Study Bible NIV Deut. 30:11:15:19] but each can be narrowed down very explicitly..."Now what I am commanding you today is not too difficult for you or beyond your reach... See, I set before you today life and prosperity, death and destruction.. I command you today to love the Lord your God, to walk in his ways, and to keep his commands, decrees, and statutes; then you will live and increase, and the Lord your God will Bless you in the land you are entering to possess. But if your heart turns away and you are not obedient, and you are drawn away to bow down to other gods and worship them. I declare to you this day you will be destroyed......... This day I call heaven and earth as witnesses against you that I have set before you life and death, blessings and curses. Now choose life so that you and your children may live......listen to his voice so you may hold fast to him."

Pretty straightforward if you ask me! God made it very clear to Moses that he was a jealous God and would not tolerate any form of worship to any other image or object. He also made it very clear that He and He alone was the one true God and creator of the Universe. He has also proven time and time again He is a very patient God....slow to anger, and quick to forgive. Again, as expressed in numerous places throughout the Old and New Testaments.

Chronicles 2:7 tells us God said ... "If my people, who are called by my name, will humble themselves and seek my face and turn from their wicked ways, then I will hear from the heavens, and forgive their sin and heal their land...."

We must do more than acknowledge the sinful ways of this nation. We must refuse to bow to any man-made law that goes against God. For we answer to God, not man. And we must NEVER forget that. Too many, I believe have done just that, forgotten who they ultimately are accountable to and not just for what we have done but what we have failed to do. Dietrich Bonhoeffer tried to warn the Church Leaders during the rise of the Hitler Nazi Regime, "Silence in the face of Evil is itself Evil. God will not hold us guiltless. Not to speak is to speak. Not to act is to act." For those of you who don't know, Pastor Bonhoeffer was martyred just weeks before the liberation of Germany. Edmund Burke advised, "The only thing necessary for the triumph of evil is for good men to do nothing." And C.S. Lewis told us, "To walk out of God's will is to step into nowhere."

I don't expect the federal government to save us. They intentionally destroyed us. And I know One election cycle can not undo the damages and erosion that has occurred over the past 70 years. And a few dozen people finally leaving their elected positions is not the answer.

The only answer is a change of heart among the millions of people who call themselves American Citizens. Especially those People who say they believe in God. And are no longer willing to hide it from the public square. People who are no longer willing to tolerate being told that their faith and their religious beliefs must be confined to the four walls of their homes. Or their places of worship. Refusing to be told it is unacceptable to discuss religion or politics other than in a private setting. Where there is no "risk of offending another person." Especially when members of Congress are given a bullhorn to use on the steps of The Capitol. Defending acts of terrorism. Against our nation on 9/11 and against the Jewish people on 10/7. Or the steps of our Supreme Court, with no pushback. Not even when it is an open attempt from the leader of the Senate majority to harass and threaten members of the judicial branch of the government. Because he and his colleagues are angry with a decision, in direct opposition to one of their beliefs. Disparaging one form of religion. Creating friction among citizens over religious beliefs. Holding a firm belief that there is no God. Or no One True God, is in and of itself promoting a preferred tolerated form of religion. By implying the preference that America should have no religion at all. Something our federal government is NOT permitted to do. Yet have almost succeeded in accomplishing. More people with the microphone tote that we are a secular nation than people who hold to our Christian-Judeo founding.

The silent majority needs to not only refuse to remain silent, they need to be willing to step up to the plate and once again make their voices known. We have allowed the power of the public opinion to be dominated by the mob's point of view. A mob who, in too many instances, openly opposes God. Denouncing His definition of good and evil, right and wrong, far too long. When that very first Supreme Court case ruling against our right to openly express our belief in God was handed down went unchallenged, and far too many people of faith chose to take on a defensive attitude. Believing it would be safer to keep their faith as a private affair between them and their God. In the hopes of going unnoticed, not willing or wanting to make any waves, upset the apple cart: or heaven forbid, be accused of trying to impose their beliefs onto others! Er go the birth of the period where it was believed it better and wiser to never discuss religion or politics in public! Don't give the government cause to come after us. Forgetting they ARE THE GOVERNMENT in the eyes of Our Constitution.

It's become pretty easy to see just how much of a failure that approach has proven to be. And it definitely was not the approach we, as believers, were instructed to do. "Go ye forth into the nations and make disciples of all nations." We've become unwilling to even go into our own nation. We don't want to take it beyond the doors of our home or place of worship. "Let Him send someone else! I want people to like me. It's not my job to challenge them." How sad! Well, guess what? According to the bible, it is your job. If you say, you are walking with God. When you are called to give an account of your life, as stated earlier, you will be judged on what you have done and what you have failed to do. Have you chosen to help a lost soul find his way, or did you direct him to the gates of hell? Or did you just leave him to wander to find his own way?

Did you know the command to "fear not" actually appears in the Bible 365 times, a very interesting coincidence the same number of days in our calendar.

Let's take a look at what Isaiah 41:10 has to say....."Fear not, for I am with you; do not be dismayed, for I am your God; I will strengthen you. I will help you. I will uphold you with my righteous right hand.`

And again, let's take a look at the very last line of Matthew's Gospel account, they were instructed to go and make disciples of all nations, teaching them "to obey everything I have commanded you. And surely I will be with you always, to the end of the age."

And what does that really mean? Not only has the Father been with us, but so has The Son and The Holy Spirit, Jesus had promised to send when He returned to the Father.

Over and over again, in numerous ways throughout the Bible, we have been commanded not to conform to the ways of this broken world. Be the light in the darkness. Be the salt of the earth, slow down the natural decay. But time after time between the nineteen sixties and now, with each misconstrued interpretation of the First Amendment, written to tell the elected they can never tell us how we are permitted to worship, we have been forced to choose between obeying the Word of God and conforming to the demands of this broken secular world. And far too many times, we as a nation chose wrongly and yielded to the demands of a broken secular world. Do not cling to the notion that because God loves everyone, He likes or approves of our behavior or actions. That is the farthest thing from the truth. Yes, God loves us with an everlasting love. But IF God didn't care what we did, He would have not been bound to watch His Beloved Son suffer and die for our actions.

Here in America, it has taken more than 200 years to challenge us regarding true freedom of expression in all matters. Especially those pertaining to God. And make no mistake, we are being challenged. We are under assault. Or, more accurately, God is under assault [has been since March of 1962] and, therefore, anyone who believes in His existence.

I believe it's obvious where I stand. I stand with God. Because I know as long as I stand with and for my God...My God stands with and for me. We were told... "What shall we then say to these things? If God be for us, who can be against us?"

Now you know - where I stand with God

So, I would like to move on while remaining within the context of that very important First Amendment: not only are we guaranteed free speech. ... our Founding Fathers gave us the right to use it to petition the Government for a redress of grievances we have against them. Nowhere in the history of mankind has a commoner been granted the right to address a grievance against those in power.

Yet this is exactly what Our Founding Fathers told them we have the right to do.

Chapter Two
Why I Can Not Support the Democratic Party: My Grievances

"Heavenly Father..... Help me endure the uncertainty of tomorrow and live for You today in Your Peace."

I cannot support, honor or comply with the current president, Joseph Biden, or his administration because doing so goes against My God. His laws, decrees and commands. And God is the Ultimate Higher authority to whom we all must answer. Including and especially all who rise to positions of authority for a limited period of time. I quoted Luke 12:48 earlier. They have been given much! We have individuals who were elected into representative positions within both Chambers of our federal government who are well into their seventies and eighties and one who is ninety years of age. We also have had a few individuals who were granted a lifetime appointment within our judicial branch and stayed on the bench for more than 30 years. It is becoming painfully clear that we have people within our government who cannot relinquish their positions of power and authority. And I believe many of us have come to understand that those elected have made it exceptionally difficult, financially, to vote them out. In other words, they have managed to rig the system in their favor, not ours! For decades, they decided which people sitting at their high-stakes table would be presented to the people for consideration. No new players, no one who would break up the game!

This goes against the clear outlines of how terms in elected office were designed: Article One Section 2 ...The House of Representatives shall be composed of members chosen every second year by the People. Amendment 17 ... The Senate of the United States shall be composed of two Senators from each State, elected by the People, therefore, for six years... Article 2 Section 1... The executive Power shall be vested in a President of the United States of America... He shall hold his Office for the Term of four years. In a sincere attempt at avoiding the temptation of addiction that such a position of power could impose, Our Founding Fathers designed changes within the governmental system every two years. Congress serves 2 years. The President serves 4 years. The Senate serves 6 years. Joseph Biden served in the Senate Chamber for 36 years. The office of the Vice Presidency for 8 years. And was sworn into the office of the presidency on January 20, 2021. There are kings who haven't been in power that long! These people have been playing musical chairs, moving from one chamber to another for far too long.

The first grievance I wish to address is the current amount of Debt the federal government has heaped upon the shoulders of the American citizens. A debt that realistically can not be paid off, and those who have accumulated this debt know this to be a fact, yet they keep on adding to the number.

As of this very moment, the Debt owed by The United States of America exceeds $34 Trillion Dollars, a number that increases, along with interest, every single day. And yet another outrageous spending bill cleared the House, heaping another $1.2 Trillion into the pot. For the sake of perspective, it takes nine 0's after a number to make up a trillion dollars. Will these people ever run out of 0's? They are not spending Monopoly Money. They are spending your great-grandchildren's money. And they do not care! Because what they have done will never impact the lives of their children or grandchildren. They made certain of that!

This is unacceptable, unsustainable and out and out wreckless on behalf of the people currently in our federal government, most of whom will never have to face the responsibility of tackling how to genuinely address how to pay it down. That means at the current time in our history the government has placed just about $95,000 worth of credit upon all 337 million citizens currently on our census. Let's put this into perspective: Every man, woman, and child will be held accountable for that much debt! Except, of course, those responsible for it. They will just keep adding to it through the hefty pensions and health benefits they've granted themselves for life. How many future generations will be forced to send money to them through the IRS system just so the government can continue to pay off the interest, which will climb with the debt ... this past fiscal year ending in September 2023, our government was required to pay $659 Billion dollars worth of interest on the debt our government has unabashedly accumulated. A figure up $184 billion more than in 2022 and nearly double what it was in 2020 when Mr. Joseph Biden took office. These are staggering numbers, and this person keeps demanding Congress give him more. And we know Mr. Schumer is more than willing to fight to get it for him! With no real resistance from Mr. McConnell.

Most American citizens' work week consists of 5 days, with the wages earned for the first 3 of those days automatically designated for the government in the form of taxes, local, state, and federal, government insurance plans such as unemployment or workmen's compensation. In addition, some are required to pay union dues, while others must contribute to job-supplied healthcare programs. Along with a percentage into the government's possession to be added to Social Security and Medicare accounts, American citizens will become eligible to withdraw from, at the government's designated age of retirement from the workforce. Which the government keeps changing. And that relies on whether or not you live to see the designated age when you can finally stop working and supporting THEM. Is it really any wonder millions of Americans have withdrawn from the workforce? Just got tired of all their money going everywhere except into their bank accounts and wallets to pay for their living expenses and occasional self-indulgence. Have they had it with a government that believes they are working for them? Instead of what the government is supposed to be .. a body of elected officials there to represent the people and strive to do everything to guarantee their God given rights to pursue their own happiness and prosperity!

The current estimated population of the United States is just over 337 Million citizens. Of that number, 140,000 have a net worth of at least $50 million dollars, and 724 have a worth in the Billions. This means out of 337 million people, 140,724 are extremely wealthy. In 2020, over half of the members of our Congress were millionaires. Yet these are the people who lean into the microphone and say, "The rich don't pay their fair share." While adding to their own wealth every year, they remain in office! I see a lot wrong with that whole picture. And no matter how hard I try to do a word problem to clarify this claim, I come up empty. The current tax table goes from 10 to 37%. Personally, I believe the problem does not rely on the very wealthy needing to pay more. It's the government learning they must spend less. A LOT LESS. They need to understand the only money they have to spend is what the American citizens are required by law to pay. The government itself has very few means of generating any substantial revenue. After all, it is not a business. It's an established body of citizens who took an oath to serve the people and their best interests. I don't see that happening in Washington DC, do you?

There is, in my humble opinion, the misconception that America is the wealthiest nation in the world. When the reality is that America has a rather large portion of individual citizens who are considered wealthy. America, as a nation, holds the highest amount of debt. No other country has placed that much of a financial burden onto their citizens. We have become THE Nation holding the largest amount of debt while still pretending we can financially assist any nation in need. Along with supplying the largest amount of money to fund world organizations such as WHO, NATO and the United Nations. I think it would be in the absolute interest of the 337 million American citizens if we started taking care of our own nation and the citizens of our nation first. It is ludicrous to think we should borrow money to give to other nations. It simply makes no sense!

We will always be a nation God blessed with an insurmountable amount of rich natural resources. But by no means is the nation itself wealthy. And the people in government must relinquish their misguided belief the nation has an endless amount of wealth to draw from. And accept the very harsh reality that they have bled three generations' worth of its citizens dry. The Federal Government is Bankrupt. But insists on denying that fact. And is waging war on the conservative, fiscally responsible states. For those of you unaware of who holds the largest portion of debt our federal government has abound, we, the people, hold 74%. Then comes Japan. With China building on the holdings of its associated territories, the undisputed largest holder of America's debt. Don't know about you, but that scares me!

In the year 2023, our federal government budgeted $60.4 Billion Dollars in aid to 10 foreign countries... Bilateral aid to Ukraine between January 24, 2022, and May 31, 2023, exceeded $76 Billion dollars. And Mr. Biden keeps telling us they must have more. And a piece of information you may not know: if the Bill Mr. Schumer and Mr. McConnell are pushing makes it to the president's desk, it guarantees the United States will continue to fund this war through the year 2026. I don't understand how this can be justified. Knowing these packages are placing an additional financial burden onto the shoulders of future generations of American citizens that have yet to be born. Not to mention such a piece of legislation would require a different viewpoint and need congressional approval to reverse course.

This is the first major grievance I have against this administration. The fact that they are willfully and intentionally placing an insurmountable amount of debt onto American citizens, including the unborn future generations.

And the current president has announced he will completely reject the Supreme Court's ruling regarding his desire to forgive student loan debt. This will add at least an additional $116 Billion plus onto our debt, claiming, "for far too long borrowers fell through the cracks of a broken system that failed to keep accurate track of their progress towards forgiveness," according to his US Secretary of Education, Miguel Cardona. This after doing absolutely nothing during his years in political power to stop or even question the validity of the monumental unnecessary increases in tuition and other costs associated with attending an institute of higher learning. Does that sound like creating a problem so you can pretend to fix it?

Hoping they won't question why now instead of when. Could it be seen as an attempt to "buy votes ?" For you to decide. I just know my adult children were in their thirties before they were able to pay off their debt. And that millions of adults their age shouldn't be held responsible for anyone else's debt. Especially those who long to assist their own children who may choose to further their education after High School.

In essence, this administration is determined to throw the consequences of the blatant failures of previous administrations [Biden himself was a part of] and government bureaucrats onto the citizens of our nation.

Another major grievance I have against this administration is how they willfully chose to abandon their responsibility to uphold the country's laws regarding immigration. As well as ignoring their obligation to protect each state against invasion. Which is happening all along our southern border! Which, in effect, is impacting every state within our country. Not just the states they are entering into illegally.

The most important function of our federal government is to ensure the national security of our nation. This responsibility is not being taken seriously when the Executive Branch of our government is fully aware of the fact that millions upon millions of people from around the globe continue to break our immigration laws and enter our country illegally. On a daily basis. Choosing to continue to allow this invasion to happen is a complete dereliction of duty. It clearly states in Article IV Section. 4. that The United States shall guarantee to every State in this union a Republican form of government [they use the word republican because we are a Constitutional Republic, NOT A DEMOCRACY] and shall protect each of them against invasion...... and against domestic violence.

A broken border is a broken immigration system. And this system is currently broken solely because the democrats in power are willfully choosing to ignore the laws. Laws duly established by the representative voices of the governed. Who stated they want to control the number of immigrants permitted to enter into our nation on each given year. By allowing people from foreign countries to break our laws, all of which is resulting in unthinkable acts of violence on display, as well as hidden from view, is again a complete dereliction of duty by not doing everything possible to ward off domestic violence.

Their choice and lack of action to correct what they know is broken, is resulting in extreme hardships on the American citizens. Citizens who are being forced to take on the financial responsibilities incurred through the housing, medical, educational and basic day-to-day living necessities, all of which are needed to meet the immediate needs of thousands of people a day at a time in our country when their own citizens are struggling themselves to make ends meet. This is just wrong. These people hide behind the lie that they are being charitable and doing good. When in reality, they demand we give them money so they can make themselves feel good. Forgetting that we, the citizens of the United States, are their immediate neighbors. Their immediate and first responsibility. And that they should love us as they love themselves! If they want to operate under God's command to love thy neighbor as thyself, they should be looking at their neighbors right here before searching out and prioritizing neighbors in other nations.

And as if that isn't bad enough, these democrats continue to throw billions of dollars to foreign leaders under the pretext that poor countries need to be taken care of! Well, I think it's pretty safe to say the leaders are NOT USING THE MONEY we supply to them for humanitarian purposes. If they were, their citizens wouldn't still be leaving in droves! To head here, to America, where they have been convinced is flowing with milk and honey for the taking… not to buy but to be handed out freely at the expense of America's citizens... And now, American citizens are being displaced to house illegal immigrants.

And how many of these immigrants are being forced into illegal forms of slavery to pay off the exorbitant amount of money the cartels charge to make that dangerous journey to so-called freedom.?

How many American families are subjected to the loss of a loved one as a result of the tons of illegal drugs that make it into our country? Solely because the federal government chooses to prevent it from happening? How many more acts of violence committed by an illegal immigrant against an American citizen are we going to be forced to accept?

How many ranchers and residents along our southern border states must live in constant fear of the criminals who have seized control of an intentionally unprotected area of our nation?

How can the very nation that fought the civil war to abolish the notion that any human being could be owned, accept the stain of all stains in the eyes of God, and acknowledge that they facilitated in the disappearance of 84,000 innocent unaccompanied children by simply relinquishing them to the unknown adult that answered the phone number pinned onto their shirt? Is it because they consider them a minor? Have we once again been reduced to identifying a human being as a thing.... unworthy of our protection? I do not think that is how God views them. According to Jesus, we are warned, "Whoever causes one of these little ones who believe in Me to sin, it would be better for him if a millstone were hung around his neck, and he were drowned in the depth of the sea."

I believe the following statement from the Bible can very easily be applied to our current federal government. How they are doing nothing to prevent the horrors of child sexual exploitation. An act that has resulted in The United States of America having the highest demand to purchase young children to satisfy the wicked, evil desires of adults. And that Mexican government leaders are turning a blind eye to the cartels more than willing to supply those poor, innocent children for the right price. ..... The reference is taken from Matthew 18:6: "We are all human, so offenses will happen, but our Savior pronounces woe on the person who offends and causes others to sin. Anyone who leads others into sin bears a deep-seated wickedness that attempts to confuse and destroy another's potential." How many lives, innocent young lives, are these two governments destroying by simply turning a blind eye instead of doing everything possible to prevent such atrocities against children from occurring.

How many lives are being destroyed by such callous neglect on behalf of the government of the United States? How long can this be tolerated? The millions of people the government insists on labeling "undocumented" or the newest catchphrase, "Newcomers," are people just like the current administration. They are showing total disrespect for the laws of the Nation; they have entered illegally. And referring to them as undocumented or any other phrase they invent will never change the fact that those people have committed a crime against our nation. Nor will it change the fact that the current federal administration is an accessory to that crime by openly participating and encouraging the crime.

Martin Luther King Jr. stated, "To ignore evil is to be an accomplice to it." And long before Martin Luther King Jr., Aleksandr Solzhenitsyn said, "Evil people always support each other; that is their chief strength" And Terry Pratchett warned, "Evil begins when you begin to treat people as things." And unfortunately, this nation began treating a newly conceived infant as "a thing" decades ago, and now it refers to a child that illegally entered our country without any identification as an "unaccompanied minor."

God help the Innocent Children, and Shame on us for not!

Another major grievance I have is the out-and-out abuse of power while holding the office of the presidency through the continual stream of "Executive Orders." So many on his very first day in office that created this out-of-control invasion of our country.

Instead of being seen as the ultimate privilege, it has become the acceptable approach of enacting anything and everything that doesn't stand a chance of becoming the law of the land through the legislative process as outlined in Our Constitution.

The very first Article of Our Constitution clearly states that.. ALL legislative powers herein granted shall be vested in a Congress of the United States.

THAT statement, my friends, is THE SOLE CONCEPT OF A SELF-GOVERNING NATION! Something that had NEVER been tried before in the history of mankind! And I applaud the thought process of the men who painstakingly adopted this concept, again using the Bible as its ultimate guide.

Section. 2. Article One explains how to accomplish this newly formed idea. Structured with three separate yet equal powers of government established to guarantee that no singular branch ever succeeds in bypassing the VOICE OF THE GOVERNED!

THE HOUSE OF REPRESENTATIVES SHALL BE COMPOSED OF MEMBERS CHOSEN every second year BY THE PEOPLE OF the several states..... it then goes on to list the qualifications necessary. It also indicates that THE HOUSE will be the most numerous of the branches. Another little footnote for your thought process. For those of you scratching your heads and trying to figure out what the end game is for letting more than eleven million illegal immigrants just enter since Biden took office. A number, by the way, that exceeds the population of three of our states. Whether or not the millions upon millions of illegal immigrants ever are granted the ultimate privilege that belongs to the people of the first self-governing nation, the right to choose their leaders. They are, in fact, impacting our House of Representatives. Because the Democrats demanded all people be included in our census count. Claiming it was for the purpose of proper allocations to the individual states. And the number of representatives permitted for each county is determined by the number of people counted via the census. Not by the number of American citizens. As it should be. Only American citizens are entitled to representation in our government. Not the likes of people who are here illegally and have committed violent acts against an American Citizen. But this is another way they have been able to tilt things in their favor. That's why so many are strategically situated in predominantly democratic areas. The Democrats have already gained at least thirteen additional seats in the House of Representatives since the 2020 census. At the rate they are going if that census rule counting all people, instead of only American citizens, is still in effect when 2030 rolls around. Game over. They win. We lose! To people here illegally, who didn't even cast a vote…. Slick! Dirty! And Intentional.

The men who formulated the very complex fabric of the design of how a self-governing nation could exist based the entire concept on a bottom-up structure. Starting with the voice of the people, in a large outer circle, being given the freedom to use their voice. Through the act of freely choosing who they believed they could trust to represent them and their best interests and the best interests of the area in which they lived. Large circle, small inner circle contained by the large outer circle!

The Founding Fathers understood the differences between the needs of those who chose to reside within the cities that had become well-established. And those who chose to reside outside the larger populated areas. Which was how our country increased and expanded. They knew and understood the printer's needs far differed from that of the farmer. The design also encouraged an entrepreneurial culture. And worked diligently to come up with the proper ways of addressing those issues on a very personal state-by-state level. The precise horizontal design within the circle. Yet still contained by the people the largest element of the circle! Something no king ever concerned himself with. In their eyes all were his subjects and had no voice in the matters of how they could be treated. It was always on the whims of the Ruler.

Folks, we are still a nation of cities and towns, farmers and businesses, entrepreneur risk takers and average run-of-the-mill citizens. Living in rural and or heavily populated areas, each coming with their own needs from THEIR GOVERNMENT. And entitled to equal representation as guaranteed by Our Constitution.

Yet I believe many would agree that the government on both some State levels and definitely the Federal level has lost sight of this fact. Some Democrat-controlled states are more than happy to yield their constitutional power to the federal government for various reasons. First, they share the same viewpoint that the federal government should have the final say on how all American citizens should live. And they are more than willing to accept the strings attached to the monies the federal government sends back to them. Not really caring or interested that they could, in fact, save their residents' taxation burdens if they were willing to resume their constitutional authority, they would not be required to forfeit as much of their constituents money and freedoms to the federal government as they do.

And with regards to the federal government, how can the people maintain their voice concerning pieces of legislation thousands of pages in length, drafted by select committee members, presented to the full HOUSE demanding a vote be taken within a few days time.

The entire point of having a voice in Our Congress is to be able to reach out to our representatives after having been given the opportunity to review proposed legislation so they know how their personal constituents want them to vote for what is being proposed that will impact their lives, and communities, and states.

This doesn't happen anymore. This means the federal government is determined to run our country with, at best, very little concern over what the majority of citizens think or want. It is no longer about us, we, the people! Again, for those of you unaware of the political makeup of the United States, 27 States currently have Republican Governors. Democrats hold 23 Governor Seats. Yet the cry of the democratic party is that the majority of Americans agree with them. Numbers do not lie. That Statement is a lie meant to deceive.

Is it really any wonder there are now so many alphabet agencies and agencies developed within those agencies [many of which were implemented by executive fiat under the guise of an unconstitutional Executive Order] that many members of our congressional body don't even know they exist? Does any current member of Congress really know everything that is in The Affordable Care Act or The Patriot Act? Or any of the massive pieces of legislation imposed because of the COVID virus? Doubt it! And can we ever forget the statement then Speaker of the House Nancy Pelosi said to the full house regarding the Affordable Care Act, "We need to pass it to see what's in it." And the worst part about it, the democrats did what she told them to do. And we're still finding out what's in that massive piece of legislation that concerns our health care. And how the hospitals, medical professionals, pharmaceutical industry and insurance companies negotiated what to do regarding our health. How to do it, what to charge all concerned parties, how they could bill the patient…. And I'll stop there because if you don't see the point, you never will!

It is past time to reign in the heavy hand of our federal government. It is past time to demand Our Constitution once again become the RULING GUIDELINES OF OUR NATION. It is time the federal government understands its role within the outlined organizational body of how a self-governing nation is to operate... from the BOTTOM UP AND NOT FROM THE TOP DOWN. IT IS TIME ONCE AGAIN FOR THE FEDERAL GOVERNMENT TO ACCEPT THE VERY LIMITED POWER AND AUTHORITY OUR CONSTITUTION ENTRUSTED TO THEM ON BEHALF OF THE STATES. Always taking into consideration all of the citizens who inhabit all of the states. And never governing for the portion of people who got them elected. Side note: I believe it's past time to purge the Capital of Lobbyists. After all, it is The People's House and should only be occupied by the people we send there to represent us.

It is time the members of our federal government be reminded that THE STATES CREATED A FEDERAL BRANCH OF THE GOVERNMENT for very specific limited reasons. And it was

NEVER INTENDED TO IMPOSE, RESTRICT, LIMIT OR DEFINE HOW THE AMERICAN CITIZENS COULD EXIST. Especially in their own states. Nor should it ever challenge the decisions of a State's duly elected legislative body. When they are governing and enacting legislation to meet the needs and voiced objectives of their people. Especially when it is what the people of that state request from its representatives. Unless we as a nation ever find ourselves once again in a gridlock over an issue as divisive and immorally offensive as slavery. Never because it differs from the opinions, views, or agenda of a current ruling political party in the Nation's Capital.

Our federal government has expanded itself in such a manner over the decades and has become so large in scope that it is impossible for our elected officials to really have a full insight or the wherewithal to perform the necessary task of oversight into how these agencies are running. What they are actually doing, and whether or not they are overstepping their position within the government. Many of the current rules, regulations, and stipulations we have accepted and heed are actually illegal. Because they were never imposed through the legislative process. These agencies can make all the suggestions and recommendations they want. But they do not have the authority to tell us what to do. What is acceptable to them is meaningless if we disagree. That is the whole point of being free people. Entrusted to make our own decisions. I do not have the right to tell my neighbor what type of appliance they should own.

How hot they should set their water heater. ETC.ETC. Time once again for our congress to determine how many of these agencies represent the best interests of The American citizens ... And if not, time to defund and dismantle them. Especially those agencies that have become a real hindrance to our freedoms. And this nonsense of an agency determining they are going to develop a subdivision [fancy way of establishing yet another agency we will be handed the paystubs for] within their own agency has got to stop. It is time for real, meaningful oversight to determine if the money allotted in the federal budgets for the continued funding of these agencies can still be justified? Unfortunately, they are all government employees, so we're stuck with their pensions anyway; so if one element of expenditures can be eliminated I say so be it. Ease the pain, don't continue to increase it, show some mercy!

All positions within our government's structure must go back to ANSWERING TO THE PEOPLE. ALL THE PEOPLE. NOT JUST THOSE HOLDING A BULLHORN. I have numerous grievances when it comes to our federal government and how it is currently functioning. Not really happy with the approach of a few governmental bodies in more than a few of our individual states either. How they are currently being run, literally into the grown. An intentional use of words because I do not believe they are operating within the distinct description that would fall under the meaning of the word governed by the people for the people! Many innocent American citizens are trapped in crime-ridden cities with no way out. The Tenth Amendment of The Constitution reads as follows. The powers not delegated to the United States by The Constitution, nor prohibited by it to the States, are reserved to the States respectively, OR TO THE PEOPLE. Personally, I believe far too many of our elected officials are not operating within the directive of that paragraph of The Constitution while completely ignoring other passages. Our Constitution is meant to be taken as a whole, not the piecemeal we are witnessing. Let's revisit what many of them did very shortly after taking office in January of 2021, when they were still keeping the spread of the COVID virus front and center for the continued use of the fear factor they created. Since Mr. Biden was not able to keep his campaign promise of crushing it. It subtly fell by the wayside. But not before he demanded, not suggested, demanded that all American citizens, more than three months of age, take part in a drug experiment being conducted by the pharmaceutical giants. With no consideration for the American citizens to discuss the pros and cons of participating in such a venture. Do it or else. Enter intimidation, followed by shame. This attitude of governing is totally unacceptable, at least to me. It is far outside the purview of his presidential authority. And in direct conflict with Our Constitution.

Again, now you know! I also take a very negative outlook on the willingness of the federal government to be the largest contributor [with our money] to agencies that were established after the two World Wars, which the American Military was heavily involved in ending. At the time uniting, numerous countries with shared beliefs regarding issues such as how to prevent wars. How to conduct international trade, that would benefit all participating countries. As well as how to tackle world health issues. Along with a few, I don't deem it necessary for the United States to participate since they serve only those who established them. So where do we, the average American citizen, stand? On the priority list of those elected to represent us? I know where I feel I matter. That to them, I am nothing more than a person who is being forced into an overdraft over my limited financial status and that I will never live to pay anything but the very high interest rates. Unwillingly left with transferring the debt to my children, grandchildren and great-grandchildren to pick up where I left off. So, where do we go from here? What options do we really have?

The path forward: The first is coming to accept the truth that the large majority of people who have been in our Capital for decades did this to us. By imposing policies they knew would create financial hardships. Decreeing unnecessary burdens, regulations, and rules specifically designed to let them run our lives! In reality, they have created their own Very Large Plantation, and we are subject to our masters' wishes. Plainly speaking, we are right back to where we started when we declared our independence from the British Crown. And if you want to prove to yourself, read the grievances our Founding Fathers stated against the Crown. Some of these major issues, problems and policies will require generations to reverse.

After all, we've been traveling down this road of destruction since the Nineteen Sixties. Again, if you are willing to see the truth, look at the ages and lengths of time some of our representatives have been in power. Mr. Bidens' solution to everything is to give me more power, more money and more time. Personally, I believe half a century in power and more than $34 trillion dollars, plus interest, we already have to pay back is more than enough. These career politicians must concede they failed at their attempt to rewrite what our nation stands for. What role God should play in the Nation and its citizens' lives. And just step down. I'm from their generation. Have had a front-row seat as this has all unfolded. This division is not new. It began with our nation's involvement in the Vietnam War when America was willing to fight against the spread of communism. Again, three factions emerged during that era. Those willing to fight. Risk their lives. Young Soldiers who were ridiculed and shamed upon their return. Those who remained silent. And those who hated what our nation stood for and set about the task of radically changing what they despised. Many ran for and got elected to positions of power. Their way of doing things is clearly what has brought about the failure of our government. What they do is not an act of incompetence, it is intentional. And a real threat to Our Nation. It is time to completely rethink our loyalties to a political party. And make the very survival of our nation, for the next generation, The Top Priority when choosing who to select to represent us. Until those brave fifty-six men, Our Founding Fathers, said enough! We are better off on our own. There were two categories of people in the world. Rulers and subjects to be ruled as seen fit! Before the establishment of The United States of America, there was no such thing as a Citizen. You either held a position of authority to rule over people, or you were ruled by those people. With no say whatsoever over how you could live your life. It was lived for those over you. People lived to benefit those above them! To make their lives easier. Unfortunately, among those fifty-six men some were very beholden to keep a remnant of that mindset alive. And succeeded in doing so until The Civil War. They had to concede humiliating failure under the newly formed political party known as the Republican Party. Led by Abraham Lincoln, a man whom they assassinated. Out of utter, anger-driven hatred for daring to demand, they relinquish their authority to rule another person's life. Ending what had been acceptable practice throughout the world until it hit the shores of America! President Lincoln was even willing to make arrangements for any freed Persons' passage back to their homeland if they so desired. I can't help but wonder how many who chose to stay were saved from being sold a second time if they had returned to Africa and shipped to a country other than America. Before being known as the Republican party most affiliated with it were known as Federalists, or those who supported the Ratification of the Constitution. While the party Thomas Jefferson and James Madison founded has had three names so far: The Democrat-Republican party, The Jefferson Republican Party before becoming the modern Democratic Party formed from factions of the Democratic-Republican party, which, according to historians, had largely collapsed by 1824; being newly formed and founded by Martin Van Buren, from New York to elect Andrew Jackson of Tennessee. Throughout the history of the major political parties one always sought to control or interfere in the lives of the American citizen. The current Democratic party stems from the Lyndon B. Johnson vs. Barry Goldwater race. Mr. Johnson's campaign centered on his vision of creating what he referenced as A Great Society, something Mr. Goldwater strongly opposed. Many of the issues we are dealing with, and to this day, stem from his effort to completely transform and change our society. Beginning with his determination in believing he could eradicate poverty. Something that sounds wonderful. However The Bible states the poor we will always have among us. Yet many still alive from the Johnson era are still debating what his attempt to create a " Great Society" on a pro and con level, especially with regards to the demise of the family structure within the black community. Which gradually found its way into all avenues of the American family... Bishop Fulton Sheen, of the Diocese of New York from 1951-1966, warned, "If the bringing of children into the world is today an economic burden, it is because the social system is inadequate; and not because God's law is wrong. Therefore, the State should remove the causes of that burden. The human must not be limited and controlled to fit the Economic, but the Economic must be expanded to fit the human." What started back then, late Sixties early Seventies, has finally reached the unsustainable attitude of our politicians.

And must be addressed and eradicated. It is unacceptable and threatens to destroy us completely, and can not go on any further. Too many have overstayed their welcome. And failed miserably at fulfilling their duties of making sure the American citizen, Not be denied their right to pursue. Be given the opportunity of seeking a better way of life. One they are willing to work to attain. And continue striving to form a more perfect union for their children. Understanding perfection is not theirs to achieve but to never stop striving for. Currently, neither the White House, political and economic advisers, nor the media dare to say America is in a depression. However, by definition, that is exactly where the policies and outrageous debt have taken the average American Citizen. Far too many are in a depressed way of life with no way out!

Chapter Three

Here comes the difficult part. Swallowing the bitter pill of facing up to, living in and with the consequences of making a lot of bad choices. Starting with misplacing our trust in mankind instead of where it belongs. In God. The very thing we chose to write on our currency. The very thing we chose to hang above the doorways of Our House of Government. The very thing we and they lost sight of.

Then, we must accept the reality that no human being is capable of legislating a great society.

That can only be acquired when people do what God demands them to do. It is the only way. Trying anything else will only bring about what God told us would happen.

As written in Deuteronomy, two different places in two different ways. Deuteronomy 28 and again in Deuteronomy 30 where God actually calls the heavens and the earth as His witnesses against us.

He wasn't messing around. Very straightforward. Either by His way or on our own. From what I'm observing, choosing the latter is not working at all!

Neither is relying on mankind!

I think it's time to be realistic and change course, back to doing things His way so He can willfully bestow his blessings upon us.

And those who disagree have two very easy options to choose from. Find a different place to live. Or live here sharing in the prosperity brought upon the nation by those who choose to follow God!

Strongly willing to denounce people who are acting like gods. Include ourselves if we think we can pick or choose which of His commands is suitable to our viewpoints or willingness to live by!

With God, it's simply all or nothing. If you're not willing to abide by just one, you might as well walk away from him completely. And we should not be surprised. He made it very clear to the Hebrews, when he issued his commands, that he is a jealous God who will not tolerate any other god before him. It was the first order of business.

Now it's time to decide yours. Which will determine the fate of not only our nation and society but that of the free world. If you stand with God against their agenda for our nation, as I do, we are seen as potential enemies. Adversaries. It's why they hate our 2nd Amendment. As long as it stays intact, they will never be able to overtake us. Easily justifying all they do to herd us into submission. Like all cultures before us.

We are divided. Not a doubt. And my generation took it into the public square. Division that has manifested into great discord among the citizens of our nation. Which has brought about the current atmosphere of strife. Constant conflict. Strong bouts of contention.

And an open display to the indifferences of its citizens over moral issues. We have a governing body determined to redefine what is good and what is evil in the eyes of God. Desperate to establish a religion based solely on political correctness. A term that peppered the vocabulary following the Marxist Leninist movement that fueled the 1917 Russian Revolution that ushered in the politics, policies and principles of The Communist Party of the Soviet Union. There is a faction within our government who embraced that philosophy and desperately tried to convince the American people to adopt that way of life. All while benefiting from the capitalistic way of America that enabled them to become wealthy citizens. While supposedly representing the American citizens and upholding the American way of Life.

We are in the crosshairs, my friends. One generation is dying away; another is coming of age. One where many were denied true knowledge of God. His language. His Word. And have been fed a new vocabulary designed to deceive and confuse. Most of which was kept in the dark until covid shut down our schools, and parents were flabbergasted by what they saw through "remote teaching" via the internet while at home. God always finds a way to turn evil into good. For those who love him. And those He loves, I might add! Innocent children. God exposed the out-and-out wickedness young children were being subjected to through our public school system, that I can no longer refer to as an educational system. Not after seeing what they are attempting to do.

But I applaud the parents fighting back against our government, desperate to shield the vulnerable minds of four, five, six and seven-year-olds from being shown pornographic materials. Children are being encouraged to consider any and all forms of sex - sexual partners - sexual persuasion. As well as being tempted to think they can choose their sexual identity or gender. Educators, at the behest of our government, are ignoring scientific and biological facts that there are only two genders. Male and female. The children of America are not being educated. Taught how to use their God-given brains. They are being instructed by their government as to what is acceptable in the eyes of the government. Not God. Their Creator.

We must stand with the parents. Hillary Clinton, years ago, strongly stated, "It takes a village to raise a child." Well, we know, without a doubt, what village Mrs. Clinton was referring to. The village of the democratic machine. Adolf Hitler understood the only way to control Germany was to start by taking over the minds of the children. Going so far as to convince them their parents were the enemy! Now we hear Mr. Biden proclaiming, "They are OUR children." And some states have imposed laws that a child can be taken from their parents. If those parents do not comply with the [confused] minds of the children, they are responsible for poisoning. The democratic party has succeeded in creating a nation in chaos and confusion. At least with regard to school-age children in many areas. It is the democratic party who is attempting to change or alter our language. Redefine the meaning of words. The democratic party is, in fact, doing everything possible to change, modify and reinvent reality.

If you do not see this alteration taking place God help you.

Worse yet, if you do see it and do nothing about it. God help you; before it's too late. Yogi Berra said, "The future ain't what it used to be."

My generation inherited a great nation. Filled with brave men and women who'd been willing to lay down their lives for freedom's sake. I'm ashamed of what we've done to it and what we are passing on to our grandchildren. An absolute mess.

WE are living in a time when "Lonely are the Brave," and numerous cowards are willing to turn a blind eye to the evil attacks upon our nation. How many do we hear say, "Glad I'm in my eighties, don't have to struggle through this mess."

To that, I say, wow. But I know God does His finest work when everything looks lost. Prefers it, actually. Then, no man can claim the GLORY.

There is much talk these days about being on "The right side of history," whatever that really means. Since man writes history. Biblical History is a clear indicator of what that entails. Are you on God's side? Or the fallen side, in need of His redemptive mercy and grace? Are you a carryover of the era when people choose to be a "Conscious Objector," longing to remain neutral?

That time has passed, my friends. The weeds are being separated from the wheat. The great harvest of the baby boomer generation is underway. Are you planting a new harvest of seeds for The Master?

God's people of America will be saved. It's the way it's always been. It's a matter of what He has to say to you when you must give an account of your life. What did you do? To enhance and advance His Kingdom? What did you fail to do with the talents He entrusted to you?

In closing, I will state the current president of the United States does not agree with my Religious beliefs. This president and his administration does not believe I have a right to them. But that does not matter because he took an Oath to Uphold My Constitution. Each time he re-entered political office starting so, so long ago. Which means he swore to PROTECT my rights to worship My God and live under all the protections of Article 1, which gives me the freedom to exercise those beliefs. And address my grievance for redress. Therefore I can not support this man as my president because he is in direct violation of the very Oath he took when he entered into the office of the presidency.

AND I DO NOT APOLOGIZE. Nor will I yield my free will to him and his political party. He can not have my freedom, which is bestowed upon me by my creator. And I will fight to the end before surrendering the soul of our nation to him. To hand over to God's enemy. I pray you feel as strongly as I do. For if you do, you know this is not our battle. This is a battle against God. Against the Covenant, Our Founding Fathers presented to him. I choose to stand with God on this side of History. And I know I am not alone.

To be continued…to debate the battle of 1973 the battle waged against life itself!

THE DECLARATION OF INDEPENDENCE—1776 [1]

The unanimous Declaration of the thirteen united States of America

WHEN in the Course of human events, it becomes necessary for one people to dissolve the political bands which have connected them with another, and to assume among the powers of the earth, the separate and equal station to which the Laws of Nature and of Nature's God entitle them, a decent respect to the opinions of mankind requires that they should declare the causes which impel them to the separation.

[1] The delegates of the United Colonies of New Hampshire; Massachusetts Bay; Rhode Island and Providence Plantations; Connecticut; New York; New Jersey; Pennsylvania; New Castle, Kent, and Sussex, in Delaware; Maryland; Virginia; North Carolina, and South Carolina, In Congress assembled at Philadelphia, *Resolved* on the 10th of May, 1776, to recommend to the respective assemblies and conventions of the United Colonies, where no government sufficient to the exigencies of their affairs had been established, to adopt such a government as should, in the opinion of the representatives of the people, best conduce to the happiness and safety of their constituents in particular, and of America in general. A preamble to this resolution, agreed to on the 15th of May, stated the intention to be totally to suppress the exercise of every kind of authority under the British crown. On the 7th of June, certain resolutions respecting independency were moved and seconded. On the 10th of June it was resolved, that a committee should be appointed to prepare a declaration to the following effect: "That the United Colonies are, and of right ought to be, free and independent States; that they are absolved from all allegiance to the British crown; and that all political connection between them and the State of Great Britain is, and ought to be, totally dissolved." On the preceding day it was determined that the committee for preparing the declaration should consist of five, and they were chosen accordingly, in the following order: Mr. Jefferson, Mr. J. Adams, Mr. Franklin, Mr. Sherman, Mr. R. R. Livingston. On the 11th of June a resolution was passed to appoint a committee to prepare and digest the form of a confederation to be entered into between the colonies, and another committee to prepare a plan of treaties to be proposed to foreign powers. On the 12th of June, it was resolved, that a committee of Congress should be appointed by the name of a board of war and ordnance, to consist of five members. On the 25th of June, a declaration of the deputies of Pennsylvania, met in provincial conference, expressing their willingness to concur in a vote declaring the United Colonies free and independent States, was laid before Congress and read. On the 28th of June, the committee appointed to prepare a declaration of independence brought in a draught, which was read, and ordered to lie on the table. On the 1st of July, a resolution of the convention of Maryland, passed the 28th of June, authorizing the deputies of that colony to concur in declaring the United Colonies free and independent States, was laid before Congress and read. On the same day Congress resolved itself into a committee of the whole, to take into consideration the resolution respecting independency. On the 2d of July, a resolution declaring the colonies free and independent States, was adopted. A declaration to that effect was, on the same and the following days, taken into further consideration. Finally, on the 4th of July, the Declaration of Independence was agreed to, engrossed on paper, signed by John Hancock as president, and directed to be sent to the several assemblies, conventions, and committees, or councils of safety, and to the several commanding officers of the continental troops, and to be proclaimed in each of the United States, and at the head of the Army. It was also ordered to be entered upon the Journals of Congress, and on the 2d of August, a copy engrossed on parchment was signed by all but one of the fifty-six signers whose names are appended to it. That one was Matthew Thornton, of New Hampshire, who on taking his seat in November asked and obtained the privilege of signing it. Several who signed it on the 2d of August were absent when it was adopted on the 4th of July, but, approving of it, they thus signified their approbation.

NOTE.—The proof of this document, as published above, was read by Mr. Ferdinand Jefferson, the Keeper of the Rolls at the Department of State, at Washington, who compared it with the fac-simile of the original in his custody. He says: "In the fac-simile, as in the original, the whole instrument runs on without a break, but dashes are mostly inserted. I have, in this copy, followed the arrangement of paragraphs adopted in the publication of the Declaration in the newspaper of John Dunlap, and as printed by him for the Congress, which printed copy is inserted in the original Journal of the old Congress. The same paragraphs are also made by the author, in the original draught preserved in the Department of State."

We hold these truths to be self-evident, that all men are created equal, that they are endowed by their Creator with certain unalienable Rights, that among these are Life, Liberty and the pursuit of Happiness. That to secure these rights, Governments are instituted among Men, deriving their just powers from the consent of the governed,—That whenever any Form of Government becomes destructive of these ends, it is the Right of the People to alter or to abolish it, and to institute new Government, laying its foundation on such principles and organizing its powers in such form, as to them shall seem most likely to effect their Safety and Happiness. Prudence, indeed, will dictate that Governments long established should not be changed for light and transient causes; and accordingly all experience hath shewn, that mankind are more disposed to suffer, while evils are sufferable, than to right themselves by abolishing the forms to which they are accustomed. But when a long train of abuses and usurpations, pursuing invariably the same Object evinces a design to reduce them under absolute Despotism, it is their right, it is their duty, to throw off such Government, and to provide new Guards for their future security.—Such has been the patient sufferance of these Colonies; and such is now the necessity which constrains them to alter their former Systems of Government. The history of the present King of Great Britain is a history of repeated injuries and usurpations, all having in direct object the establishment of an absolute Tyranny over these States. To prove this, let Facts be submitted to a candid world.

He has refused his Assent to Laws, the most wholesome and necessary for the public good.

He has forbidden his Governors to pass Laws of immediate and pressing importance, unless suspended in their operation till his Assent should be obtained; and when so suspended, he has utterly neglected to attend to them.

He has refused to pass other Laws for the accommodation of large districts of people, unless those people would relinquish the right of Representation in the Legislature, a right inestimable to them and formidable to tyrants only.

He has called together legislative bodies at places unusual, uncomfortable, and distance

VerDate Aug 31 2005   08:33 Feb 15, 2008   Jkt 040101   PO 00000   Frm 00001   Fmt 5820   Sfmt 5820   Y:\TS\2006MAIN\2006V1.MN\V1PRE4.MN   BOB

from the depository of their public Records, for the sole purpose of fatiguing them into compliance with his measures.

He has dissolved Representative Houses repeatedly, for opposing with manly firmness his invasions on the rights of the people.

He has refused for a long time, after such dissolutions, to cause others to be elected; whereby the Legislative powers, incapable of Annihilation, have returned to the People at large for their exercise; the State remaining in the mean time exposed to all the dangers of invasion from without, and convulsions within.

He has endeavoured to prevent the population of these States; for that purpose obstructing the Laws for Naturalization of Foreigners; refusing to pass others to encourage their migrations hither, and raising the conditions of new Appropriations of Lands.

He has obstructed the Administration of Justice, by refusing his Assent to Laws for establishing Judiciary powers.

He has made Judges dependent on his Will alone, for the tenure of their offices, and the amount and payment of their salaries.

He has erected a multitude of New Offices, and sent hither swarms of Officers to harass our people, and eat out their substance.

He has kept among us, in times of peace, Standing Armies without the Consent of our legislatures.

He has affected to render the Military independent of and superior to the Civil power.

He has combined with others to subject us to a jurisdiction foreign to our constitution, and unacknowledged by our laws; giving his Assent to their acts of pretended Legislation:

For quartering large bodies of armed troops among us:

For protecting them, by a mock Trial, from punishment for any Murders which they should commit on the Inhabitants of these States:

For cutting off our Trade with all parts of the world:

For imposing Taxes on us without our Consent:

For depriving us in many cases, of the benefits of Trial by Jury:

For transporting us beyond Seas to be tried for pretended offenses:

For abolishing the free System of English Laws in a neighbouring Province, establishing therein an Arbitrary government, and enlarging its Boundaries so as to render it at once an example and fit instrument for introducing the same absolute rule into these Colonies:

For taking away our Charters, abolishing our most valuable Laws, and altering fundamentally the Forms of our Governments:

For suspending our own Legislatures, and declaring themselves invested with power to legislate for us in all cases whatsoever.

He has abdicated Government here, by declaring us out of his Protection and waging War against us.

He has plundered our seas, ravaged our Coasts, burnt our towns, and destroyed the lives of our people.

He is at this time transporting large Armies of foreign Mercenaries to compleat the works of death, desolation and tyranny, already begun with circumstances of Cruelty & perfidy scarcely paralleled in the most barbarous ages, and totally unworthy the Head of a civilized nation.

He has constrained our fellow Citizens taken Captive on the high Seas to bear Arms against their Country, to become the executioners of their friends and Brethren, or to fall themselves by their Hands.

He has excited domestic insurrections amongst us, and has endeavoured to bring on the inhabitants of our frontiers, the merciless Indian Savages, whose known rule of warfare, is an undistinguished destruction of all ages, sexes and conditions.

In every stage of these Oppressions We have Petitioned for Redress in the most humble terms: Our repeated Petitions have been answered only by repeated injury. A Prince, whose character is thus marked by every act which may define a Tyrant, is unfit to be the ruler of a free people.

Nor have We been wanting in attentions to our Brittish brethren. We have warned them from time to time of attempts by their legislature to extend an unwarrantable jurisdiction over us. We have reminded them of the circumstances of our emigration and settlement here. We have appealed to their native justice and magnanimity, and we have conjured them by the ties of our common kindred to disavow these usurpations, which, would inevitably interrupt our connections and correspondence. They too have been deaf to the voice of justice and of consanguinity. We must, therefore, acquiesce in the necessity, which denounces our Separation, and hold them, as we hold the rest of mankind, Enemies in War, in Peace Friends.

WE, THEREFORE, the Representatives of the UNITED STATES OF AMERICA, in General Congress, Assembled, appealing to the Supreme Judge of the world for the rectitude of our intentions, do, in the Name, and by Authority of the good People of these Colonies, solemnly publish and declare, That these United Colonies are, and of Right ought to be FREE AND INDEPENDENT STATES; that they are Absolved from all Allegiance to the British Crown, and that all political connection between them and the State of Great Britain, is and ought to be totally dissolved; and that as Free and Independent States, they have full Power to levy War, conclude Peace, contract Alliances, establish Commerce, and to do all other Acts and Things which Independent States may of right do. And for the support of this Declaration, with a firm reliance on the protection of divine Providence, we mutually pledge to each other our Lives, our Fortunes and our sacred Honor.

JOHN HANCOCK.

New Hampshire

JOSIAH BARTLETT,   MATTHEW THORNTON.
WM. WHIPPLE,

Massachusetts Bay

SAML. ADAMS,   ROBT. TREAT PAINE,
JOHN ADAMS,   ELBRIDGE GERRY.

Rhode Island

STEP. HOPKINS,   WILLIAM ELLERY.

VerDate Aug 31 2005   08:33 Feb 15, 2008   Jkt 040101   PO 00000   Frm 00002   Fmt 5820   Sfmt 5807   Y:\TS\2006MAIN\2006V1.MN\V1PRE4.MN   BOB

Connecticut

ROGER SHERMAN,	WM. WILLIAMS,
SAM'EL HUNTINGTON,	OLIVER WOLCOTT.

New York

WM. FLOYD,	FRANS. LEWIS,
PHIL. LIVINGSTON,	LEWIS MORRIS.

New Jersey

RICHD. STOCKTON,	JOHN HART,
JNO. WITHERSPOON,	ABRA. CLARK.
FRAS. HOPKINSON,	

Pennsylvania

ROBT. MORRIS,	JAS. SMITH,
BENJAMIN RUSH,	GEO. TAYLOR,
BENJA. FRANKLIN,	JAMES WILSON,
JOHN MORTON,	GEO. ROSS.
GEO. CLYMER,	

Delaware

CAESAR RODNEY,	THO. M'KEAN.
GEO. READ,	

Maryland

SAMUEL CHASE,	CHARLES CARROLL OF
WM. PACA,	Carrollton.
THOS. STONE,	

Virginia

GEORGE WYTHE,	THOS. NELSON, jr.,
RICHARD HENRY LEE,	FRANCIS LIGHTFOOT
TH. JEFFERSON,	LEE,
BENJA. HARRISON,	CARTER BRAXTON.

North Carolina

WM. HOOPER,	JOHN PENN.
JOSEPH HEWES,	

South Carolina

THOS. HEYWARD,	THOMAS LYNCH, Junr.,
Junr.,	ARTHUR MIDDLETON.
EDWARD RUTLEDGE,	

Georgia

BUTTON GWINNETT,	GEO. WALTON.
LYMAN HALL,	

NOTE.—Mr. Ferdinand Jefferson, Keeper of the Rolls in the Department of State, at Washington, says: "The names of the signers are spelt above as in the fac-simile of the original, but the punctuation of them is not always the same; neither do the names of the States appear in the fac-simile of the original. The names of the signers of each State are grouped together in the fac-simile of the original, except the name of Matthew Thornton, which follows that of Oliver Wolcott."

VerDate Aug 31 2005   08:33 Feb 15, 2008   Jkt 040101   PO 00000   Frm 00003   Fmt 5820   Sfmt 5800   Y:\TS\2006MAIN\2006V1.MN\V1PRE4.MN   BOB

THE
CONSTITUTION
of the United States

We the People of the United States, in Order to form a more perfect Union, establish Justice, insure domestic Tranquility, provide for the common defence, promote the general Welfare, and secure the Blessings of Liberty to ourselves and our Posterity, do ordain and establish this Constitution for the United States of America

Article. I.

SECTION. 1

All legislative Powers herein granted shall be vested in a Congress of the United States, which shall consist of a Senate and House of Representatives.

SECTION. 2

The House of Representatives shall be composed of Members chosen every second Year by the People of the several States, and the Electors in each State shall have the Qualifications requisite for Electors of the most numerous Branch of the State Legislature.

No Person shall be a Representative who shall not have attained to the Age of twenty five Years, and been seven Years a Citizen of the United States, and who shall not, when elected, be an Inhabitant of that State in which he shall be chosen.

[Representatives and direct Taxes shall be apportioned among the several States which may be included within this Union, according to their respective Numbers, which shall be determined by adding to the whole Number of free Persons, including those bound to Service for a Term of Years, and excluding Indians not taxed, three fifths of all other Persons.]* The actual Enumeration shall be made within three Years after the first Meeting of the Congress of the United States, and within every subsequent Term of ten Years, in such Manner as they shall by Law direct. The Number of Representatives shall not exceed one for every thirty Thousand, but each State shall have at Least one Representative; and until such enumeration shall be made, the State of New Hampshire shall be entitled to chuse three, Massachusetts eight, Rhode-Island and Providence Plantations one, Connecticut five, New-York six, New Jersey four, Pennsylvania eight, Delaware one, Maryland six, Virginia ten, North Carolina five, South Carolina five, and Georgia three.

When vacancies happen in the Representation from any State, the Executive Authority thereof shall issue Writs of Election to fill such Vacancies.

The House of Representatives shall chuse their Speaker and other Officers; and shall have the sole Power of Impeachment.

SECTION. 3

The Senate of the United States shall be composed of two Senators from each State, [chosen by the Legislature thereof,]* for six Years; and each Senator shall have one Vote.

Immediately after they shall be assembled in Consequence of the first Election, they shall be divided as equally as may be into three Classes. The Seats of the Senators of the first Class shall be vacated at the Expiration of the second Year, of the second Class at the Expiration of the fourth Year, and of the third Class at the Expiration of the sixth Year, so that one third may be chosen every second Year; [and if Vacancies happen by Resignation, or otherwise, during the Recess of the Legislature of any State, the Executive thereof may make temporary Appointments until the next Meeting of the Legislature, which shall then fill such Vacancies.]*

No Person shall be a Senator who shall not have attained to the Age of thirty Years, and been nine Years a Citizen of the United States, and who shall not, when elected, be an Inhabitant of that State for which he shall be chosen

The Vice President of the United States shall be President of the Senate, but shall have no Vote, unless they be equally divided.

The Senate shall chuse their other Officers, and also a President pro tempore, in the Absence of the Vice President, or when he shall exercise the Office of President of the United States

The Senate shall have the sole Power to try all Impeachments. When sitting for that Purpose, they shall be on Oath or Affirmation. When the President of the United States is tried, the Chief Justice shall preside: And no Person shall be convicted without the Concurrence of two thirds of the Members present.

Judgment in Cases of Impeachment shall not extend further than to removal from Office, and disqualification to hold and enjoy any Office of honor, Trust or Profit under the United States: but the Party convicted shall nevertheless be liable and subject to Indictment, Trial, Judgment and Punishment, according to Law.

SECTION. 4

The Times, Places and Manner of holding Elections for Senators and Representatives, shall be prescribed in each State by the Legislature thereof; but the Congress may at any time by Law make or alter such Regulations, except as to the Places of chusing Senators.

The Congress shall assemble at least once in every Year, and such Meeting shall be [on the first Monday in December,]* unless they shall by Law appoint a different Day.

SECTION. 5.

Each House shall be the Judge of the Elections, Returns and Qualifications of its own Members, and a Majority of each shall constitute a Quorum to do Business; but a smaller Number may adjourn from day to day, and may be authorized to compel the Attendance of absent Members, in such Manner, and under such Penalties as each House may provide.

Each House may determine the Rules of its Proceedings, punish its Members for disorderly Behaviour, and, with the Concurrence of two thirds, expel a Member.

Each House shall keep a Journal of its Proceedings, and from time to time publish the same, excepting such Parts as may in their Judgment require Secrecy; and the Yeas and Nays of the Members of either House on any question shall, at the Desire of one fifth of those Present, be entered on the Journal.

Neither House, during the Session of Congress, shall, without the Consent of the other, adjourn for more than three days, nor to any other Place than that in which the two Houses shall be sitting.

SECTION. 6

The Senators and Representatives shall receive a Compensation for their Services, to be ascertained by Law, and paid out of the Treasury of the United States. They shall in all Cases, except Treason, Felony and Breach of the Peace, be privileged from Arrest during their Attendance at the Session of their respective Houses, and in going to and returning from the same; and for any Speech or Debate in either House, they shall not be questioned in any other Place.

No Senator or Representative shall, during the Time for which he was elected, be appointed to any civil Office under the Authority of the United States, which shall have been created, or the Emoluments whereof shall have been encreased during such time; and no Person holding any Office under the United States, shall be a Member of either House during his Continuance in Office.

SECTION. 7

All Bills for raising Revenue shall originate in the House of Representatives; but the Senate may propose or concur with Amendments as on other Bills

Every Bill which shall have passed the House of Representatives and the Senate, shall, before it become a Law, be presented to the President of the United States; If he approve he shall sign it, but if not he shall return it, with his Objections to that House in which it shall have originated, who shall enter the Objections at large on their Journal, and proceed to reconsider it. If after such Reconsideration two thirds of that House shall agree to pass the Bill, it shall be sent, together with the Objections, to the other House, by which it shall likewise be reconsidered, and if approved by two thirds of that House, it shall become a Law. But in all such Cases the Votes of both Houses shall be determined by Yeas and Nays, and the Names of the Persons voting for and against the Bill shall be entered on the Journal of each House respectively, If any Bill shall not be returned by the President within ten Days (Sundays excepted) after it shall have been presented to him, the Same shall be a Law, in like Manner as if he had signed it, unless the Congress by their Adjournment prevent its Return, in which Case it shall not be a Law

Every Order, Resolution, or Vote to which the Concurrence of the Senate and House of Representatives may be necessary (except on a question of Adjournment) shall be presented to the President of the United States; and before the Same shall take Effect, shall be approved by him, or being disapproved by him, shall be repassed by two thirds of the Senate and House of Representatives, according to the Rules and Limitations prescribed in the Case of a Bill.

SECTION. 8

The Congress shall have Power To lay and collect Taxes, Duties, Imposts and Excises, to pay the Debts and provide for the common Defence and general Welfare of the United States; but all Duties, Imposts and Excises shall be uniform throughout the United States;

To borrow Money on the credit of the United States;

To regulate Commerce with foreign Nations, and among the several States, and with the Indian Tribes;

To establish an uniform Rule of Naturalization, and uniform Laws on the subject of Bankruptcies throughout the United States;

To coin Money, regulate the Value thereof, and of foreign Coin, and fix the Standard of Weights and Measures;

To provide for the Punishment of counterfeiting the Securities and current Coin of the United States;

To establish Post Offices and post Roads;
To promote the Progress of Science and useful Arts, by securing for limited Times to Authors and Inventors the exclusive Right to their respective Writings and Discoveries;

To constitute Tribunals inferior to the supreme Court;

To define and punish Piracies and Felonies committed on the high Seas, and Offenses against the Law of Nations;

To declare War, grant Letters of Marque and Reprisal, and make Rules concerning Captures on Land and Water;

To raise and support Armies, but no Appropriation of Money to that Use shall be for a longer Term than two Years;

To provide and maintain a Navy;

To make Rules for the Government and Regulation of the land and naval Forces;

To provide for calling forth the Militia to execute the Laws of the Union, suppress Insurrections and repel Invasions;

To provide for organizing, arming, and disciplining, the Militia, and for governing such Part of them as may be employed in the Service of the United States, reserving to the States respectively, the Appointment of the Officers, and the Authority of training the Militia according to the discipline prescribed by Congress;

To exercise exclusive Legislation in all Cases whatsoever, over such District (not exceeding ten Miles square) as may, by Cession of particular States, and the Acceptance of Congress, become the Seat of the Government of the United States, and to exercise like Authority over all Places purchased by the Consent of the Legislature of the State in which the Same shall be, for the Erection of Forts, Magazines, Arsenals, dock-Yards and other needful Buildings; -And

To make all Laws which shall be necessary and proper for carrying into Execution the foregoing Powers, and all other Powers vested by this Constitution in the Government of the United States, or in any Department or Officer thereof.

SECTION. 9

The Migration or Importation of such Persons as any of the States now existing shall think proper to admit, shall not be prohibited by the Congress prior to the Year one thousand eight hundred and eight, but a Tax or duty may be imposed on such Importation, not exceeding ten dollars for each Person

The Privilege of the Writ of Habeas Corpus shall not be suspended, unless when in Cases of Rebellion or Invasion the public Safety may require it.

No Bill of Attainder or ex post facto Law shall be passed.

[No Capitation, or other direct, Tax shall be laid, unless in Proportion to the Census or Enumeration herein before directed to be taken.]*

No Tax or Duty shall be laid on Articles exported from any State

No Preference shall be given by any Regulation of Commerce or Revenue to the Ports of one State over those of another: nor shall Vessels bound to, or from, one State, be obliged to enter, clear, or pay Duties in another.

No Money shall be drawn from the Treasury, but in Consequence of Appropriations made by Law; and a regular Statement and Account of the Receipts and Expenditures of all public Money shall be published from time to time.

No Title of Nobility shall be granted by the United States: And no Person holding any Office of Profit or Trust under them, shall, without the Consent of the Congress, accept of any present, Emolument, Office, or Title, of any kind whatever, from any King, Prince, or foreign State.

SECTION. 10

No State shall enter into any Treaty, Alliance, or Confederation; grant Letters of Marque and Reprisal; coin Money; emit Bills of Credit; make any Thing but gold and silver Coin a Tender in Payment of Debts; pass any Bill of Attainder, ex post facto Law, or Law impairing the Obligation of Contracts, or grant any Title of Nobility.

No State shall, without the Consent of the Congress, lay any Imposts or Duties on Imports or Exports, except what may be absolutely necessary for executing it's inspection Laws: and the net Produce of all Duties and Imposts, laid by any State on Imports or Exports, shall be for the Use of the Treasury of the United States; and all such Laws shall be subject to the Revision and Controul of the Congress.

No State shall, without the Consent of Congress, lay any Duty of Tonnage, keep Troops, or Ships of War in time of Peace, enter into any Agreement or Compact with another State, or with a foreign Power, or engage in War, unless actually invaded, or in such imminent Danger as will not admit of delay.

Article. II.

SECTION. 1

The executive Power shall be vested in a President of the United States of America. He shall hold his Office during the Term of four Years, and, together with the Vice President, chosen for the same Term, be elected, as follows:

Each State shall appoint, in such Manner as the Legislature thereof may direct, a Number of Electors, equal to the whole Number of Senators and Representatives to which the State may be entitled in the Congress: but no Senator or Representative, or Person holding an Office of Trust or Profit under the United States, shall be appointed an Elector.

[The Electors shall meet in their respective States, and vote by Ballot for two Persons, of whom one at least shall not be an Inhabitant of the same State with themselves. And they shall make a List of all the Persons voted for, and of the Number of Votes for each; which List they shall sign and certify, and transmit sealed to the Seat of the Government of the United States, directed to the President of the Senate. The President of the Senate shall, in the Presence of the Senate and House of Representatives, open all the Certificates, and the Votes shall then be counted. The Person having the greatest Number of Votes shall be the President, if such Number be a Majority of the whole Number of Electors appointed; and if there be more than one who have such Majority, and have an equal Number of Votes, then the House of Representatives shall immediately chuse by Ballot one of them for President; and if no Person have a Majority, then from the five highest on the List the said House shall in like Manner chuse the President. But in chusing the President, the Votes shall be taken by States, the Representation from each State having one Vote; A quorum for this Purpose shall consist of a Member or Members from two thirds of the States, and a Majority of all the States shall be necessary to a Choice. In every Case, after the Choice of the President, the Person having the greatest Number of Votes of the Electors shall be the Vice President. But if there should remain two or more who have equal Votes, the Senate shall chuse from them by Ballot the Vice President.]*

The Congress may determine the Time of chusing the Electors, and the Day on which they shall give their Votes; which Day shall be the same throughout the United States.

No Person except a natural born Citizen, or a Citizen of the United States, at the time of the Adoption of this Constitution, shall be eligible to the Office of President; neither shall any person be eligible to that Office who shall not have attained to the Age of thirty five Years, and been fourteen Years a Resident within the United States

In Case of the Removal of the President from Office, or of his Death, Resignation, or Inability to discharge the Powers and Duties of the said Office, the Same shall devolve on the Vice President, and the Congress may by Law provide for the Case of Removal, Death, Resignation or Inability, both of the President and Vice President, declaring what Officer shall then act as President, and such Officer shall act accordingly, until the Disability be removed, or a President shall be elected.]*

The President shall, at stated Times, receive for his Services, a Compensation, which shall neither be increased nor diminished during the Period for which he shall have been elected, and he shall not receive within that Period any other Emolument from the United States, or any of them.

Before he enter on the Execution of his Office, he shall take the following Oath or Affirmation:- "I do solemnly swear (or affirm) that I will faithfully execute the Office of President of the United States, and will to the best of my Ability, preserve, protect and defend the Constitution of the United States."

SECTION. 2

The President shall be Commander in Chief of the Army
and Navy of the United States, and of the Militia of the
several States, when called into the actual Service of the
United States; he may require the Opinion, in writing, of
the principal Officer in each of the executive Departments,
upon any Subject relating to the Duties of their respective
Offices, and he shall have Power to grant Reprieves and
Pardons for Offenses against the United States, except in
Cases of Impeachment.

He shall have Power, by and with the Advice and Consent
of the Senate, to make Treaties, provided two thirds of the
Senators present concur; and he shall nominate, and by and
with the Advice and Consent of the Senate, shall appoint
Ambassadors, other public Ministers and Consuls, Judges
of the supreme Court, and all other Officers of the United
States, whose Appointments are not herein otherwise
provided for, and which shall be established by Law: but
the Congress may by Law vest the Appointment of such inferior Officers, as they think proper, in the President alone,
in the Courts of Law, or in the Heads of Departments.

The President shall have Power to fill up all Vacancies
that may happen during the Recess of the Senate, by
granting Commissions which shall expire at the End of
their next Session

SECTION. 3

He shall from time to time give to the Congress Information of the State of the Union, and recommend to their
Consideration such Measures as he shall judge necessary and expedient; he may, on extraordinary Occasions,
convene both Houses, or either of them, and in Case of
Disagreement between them, with Respect to the Time of
Adjournment, he may adjourn them to such Time as he
shall think proper; he shall receive Ambassadors and other
public Ministers; he shall take Care that the Laws be faithfully executed, and shall Commission all the Officers of the
United States

SECTION. 4

The President, Vice President and all civil Officers of the
United States, shall be removed from Office on Impeachment for, and Conviction of, Treason, Bribery, or other
high Crimes and Misdemeanors.

Article. III.

SECTION. 1

The judicial Power of the United States, shall be vested in one supreme Court, and in such inferior Courts as the Congress may from time to time ordain and establish. The Judges, both of the supreme and inferior Courts, shall hold their Offices during good Behaviour, and shall at stated Times, receive for their Services, a Compensation, which shall not be diminished during their Continuance in Office.

SECTION. 2

The judicial Power shall extend to all Cases, in Law and Equity, arising under this Constitution, the Laws of the United States, and Treaties made, or which shall be made, under their Authority; - to all Cases affecting Ambassadors, other public Ministers and Consuls; - to all Cases of admiralty and maritime Jurisdiction; - to Controversies to which the United States shall be a Party; - to Controversies between two or more States; - [between a State and Citizens of another State;-]* between Citizens of different States, - between Citizens of the same State claiming Lands under Grants of different States, [and between a State, or the Citizens thereof;- and foreign States, Citizens or Subjects.]*

In all Cases affecting Ambassadors, other public Ministers and Consuls, and those in which a State shall be Party, the supreme Court shall have original Jurisdiction. In all the other Cases before mentioned, the supreme Court shall have appellate Jurisdiction, both as to Law and Fact, with such Exceptions, and under such Regulations as the Congress shall make.

The Trial of all Crimes, except in Cases of Impeachment; shall be by Jury; and such Trial shall be held in the State where the said Crimes shall have been committed; but when not committed within any State, the Trial shall be at such Place or Places as the Congress may by Law have directed.

SECTION. 3

Treason against the United States, shall consist only in levying War against them, or in adhering to their Enemies, giving them Aid and Comfort. No Person shall be convicted of Treason unless on the Testimony of two Witnesses to the same overt Act, or on Confession in open Court.

The Congress shall have Power to declare the Punishment of Treason, but no Attainder of Treason shall work Corruption of Blood, or Forfeiture except during the Life of the Person attainted

Article. IV.

SECTION. 1

Full Faith and Credit shall be given in each State to the public Acts, Records, and judicial Proceedings of every other State. And the Congress may by general Laws prescribe the Manner in which such Acts, Records and Proceedings shall be proved, and the Effect thereof.

SECTION. 2

The Citizens of each State shall be entitled to all Privileges and Immunities of Citizens in the several States
A Person charged in any State with Treason, Felony, or other Crime, who shall flee from Justice, and be found in another State, shall on Demand of the executive Authority of the State from which he fled, be delivered up, to be removed to the State having Jurisdiction of the Crime.

 No Person held to Service or Labour in one State, under the Laws thereof, escaping into another, shall, in Consequence of any Law or Regulation therein, be discharged from such Service or Labour, but shall be delivered up on Claim of the Party to whom such Service or Labour may be due.]*

SECTION. 3

New States may be admitted by the Congress into this Union; but no new State shall be formed or erected within the Jurisdiction of any other State; nor any State be formed by the Junction of two or more States, or Parts of States, without the Consent of the Legislatures of the States concerned as well as of the Congress.

The Congress shall have Power to dispose of and make all needful Rules and Regulations respecting the Territory or other Property belonging to the United States; and nothing in this Constitution shall be so construed as to Prejudice any Claims of the United States, or of any particular State.

SECTION. 4

The United States shall guarantee to every State in this Union a Republican Form of Government, and shall protect each of them against Invasion; and on Application of the Legislature, or of the Executive (when the Legislature cannot be convened) against domestic Violence.

Article. V.

The Congress, whenever two thirds of both Houses shall deem it necessary, shall propose Amendments to this Constitution, or, on the Application of the Legislatures of two thirds of the several States, shall call a Convention for proposing Amendments, which in either Case, shall be valid to all Intents and Purposes, as Part of this Constitution, when ratified by the Legislatures of three-fourths of the several States, or by Conventions in three fourths thereof, as the one or the other Mode of Ratification may be proposed by the Congress; Provided that no Amendment which may be made prior to the Year One thousand eight hundred and eight shall in any Manner affect the first and fourth Clauses in the Ninth Section of the first Article; and that no State, without its Consent, shall be deprived of its equal Suffrage in the Senate

Article. VI.

All Debts contracted and Engagements entered into, before the Adoption of this Constitution, shall be as valid against the United States under this Constitution, as under the Confederation

This Constitution, and the Laws of the United States which shall be made in Pursuance thereof; and all Treaties made, or which shall be made, under the Authority of the United States, shall be the supreme Law of the Land; and the Judges in every State shall be bound thereby, any Thing in the Constitution or Laws of any State to the Contrary notwithstanding.

The Senators and Representatives before mentioned, and the Members of the several State Legislatures, and all executive and judicial Officers, both of the United States and of the several States, shall be bound by Oath or Affirmation, to support this Constitution; but no religious Test shall ever be required as a Qualification to any Office or public Trust under the United States

Article. VII.

The Ratification of the Conventions of nine States, shall be sufficient for the Establishment of this Constitution between the States so ratifying the Same.

Done in Convention by the Unanimous Consent of the States present the Seventeenth Day of September in the Year of our Lord one thousand seven hundred and Eighty seven and of the Independence of the United States of America the Twelfth In Witness whereof We have hereunto subscribed our Names,

Go. Washington--Presidt
and deputy from Virginia

NEW HAMPSHIRE

John Langdon
Nicholas Gilman

MASSACHUSETTS

Nathaniel Gorham
Rufus King

CONNECTICUT

Wm. Saml. Johnson
Roger Sherman

NEW YORK

Alexander Hamilton

NEW JERSEY

Wil: Livingston
David Brearley
Wm. Paterson
Jona: Dayton

PENNSYLVANIA

B Franklin
Thomas Mifflin
Robt Morris
Geo. Clymer
Thos. FitzSimons
Jared Ingersoll
James Wilson
Gouv Morris

DELAWARE

Geo: Read
Gunning Bedford jun
John Dickinson
Richard Bassett
Jaco: Broom

MARYLAND

James McHenry
Dan of St. Thos. Jenifer
Danl Carroll

VIRGINIA

John Blair–
James Madison Jr.

NORTH CAROLINA

Wm. Blount
Richd. Dobbs Spaight
Hu Williamson

SOUTH CAROLINA

J. Rutledge
Charles Cotesworth Pinckney
Charles Pinckney
Pierce Butler

GEORGIA

William Few
Abr Baldwin

Attest William Jackson Secretary

In Convention Monday
September 17th, 1787.
Present
The States of
New Hampshire, Massachusetts, Connecticut, Mr. Hamilton from New York, New Jersey, Pennsylvania, Delaware, Maryland, Virginia, North Carolina, South Carolina and Georgia.

Resolved,

That the preceeding Constitution be laid before the United States in Congress assembled, and that it is the Opinion of this Convention, that it should afterwards be submitted to a Convention of Delegates, chosen in each State by the People thereof, under the Recommendation of its Legislature, for their Assent and Ratification; and that each Convention assenting to, and ratifying the Same, should give Notice thereof to the United States in Congress assembled. Resolved, That it is the Opinion of this Convention, that as soon as the Conventions of nine States shall have ratified this Constitution, the United States in Congress assembled should fix a Day on which Electors should be appointed by the States which shall have ratified the same, and a Day on which the Electors should assemble to vote for the President, and the Time and Place for commencing Proceedings under this Constitution

That after such Publication the Electors should be appointed, and the Senators and Representatives elected: That the Electors should meet on the Day fixed for the Election of the President, and should transmit their Votes certified, signed, sealed and directed, as the Constitution requires, to the Secretary of the United States in Congress assembled, that the Senators and Representatives should convene at the Time and Place assigned; that the Senators should appoint a President of the Senate, for the sole Purpose of receiving, opening and counting the Votes for President; and, that after he shall be chosen, the Congress, together with the President, should, without Delay, proceed to execute this Constitution

By the unanimous Order of the Convention

Go. Washington-Presidt:
W. JACKSON Secretary.

* Language in brackets has been changed by amendment.

THE AMENDMENTS TO THE CONSTITUTION OF THE UNITED STATES AS RATIFIED BY THE STATES

Preamble to the Bill of Rights

Congress of the United States
begun and held at the City of New-York, on
Wednesday the fourth of March,

THE Conventions of a number of the States, having at the time of their adopting the Constitution, expressed a desire, in order to prevent misconstruction or abuse of its powers, that further declaratory and restrictive clauses should be added: And as extending the ground of public confidence in the Government, will best ensure the beneficent ends of its institution

RESOLVED by the Senate and House of Representatives of the United States of America, in Congress assembled, two thirds of both Houses concurring, that the following Articles be proposed to the Legislatures of the several States, as amendments to the Constitution of the United States, all, or any of which Articles, when ratified by three fourths of the said Legislatures, to be valid to all intents and purposes, as part of the said Constitution; viz.

ARTICLES in addition to, and Amendment of the Constitution of the United States of America, proposed by Congress, and ratified by the Legislatures of the several States, pursuant to the fifth Article of the original Constitution.

(Note: The first 10 amendments to the Constitution were ratified December 15, 1791, and form what is known as the "Bill of Rights.")

Amendment I.

Congress shall make no law respecting an establishment of religion, or prohibiting the free exercise thereof; or abridging the freedom of speech, or of the press, or the right of the people peaceably to assemble, and to petition the Government for a redress of grievances.

Amendment II.

A well regulated Militia, being necessary to the security of a free State, the right of the people to keep and bear Arms, shall not be infringed.

Amendment III.

No Soldier shall, in time of peace be quartered in any house, without the consent of the Owner, nor in time of war, but in a manner to be prescribed by law.

Amendment IV.

The right of the people to be secure in their persons, houses, papers, and effects, against unreasonable searches and seizures, shall not be violated, and no Warrants shall issue, but upon probable cause, supported by Oath or affirmation, and particularly describing the place to be searched, and the persons or things to be seized.

Amendment V.

No person shall be held to answer for a capital, or otherwise infamous crime, unless on a presentment or indictment of a Grand Jury, except in cases arising in the land or naval forces, or in the Militia, when in actual service in time of War or public danger; nor shall any person be subject for the same offence to be twice put in jeopardy of life or limb; nor shall be compelled in any criminal case to be a witness against himself, nor be deprived of life, liberty, or property, without due process of law; nor shall private property be taken for public use, without just compensation.

Amendment VI.

In all criminal prosecutions, the accused shall enjoy the right to a speedy and public trial, by an impartial jury of the State and district wherein the crime shall have been committed, which district shall have been previously ascertained by law, and to be informed of the nature and cause of the accusation; to be confronted with the witnesses against him; to have compulsory process for obtaining witnesses in his favor, and to have the Assistance of Counsel for his defence.

Amendment VII.

In suits at common law, where the value in controversy shall exceed twenty dollars, the right of trial by jury shall be preserved, and no fact tried by a jury shall be otherwise re-examined in any Court of the United States, than according to the rules of the common law.

Amendment VIII.

Excessive bail shall not be required, nor excessive fines imposed, nor cruel and unusual punishments inflicted.

Amendment IX.

The enumeration in the Constitution, of certain rights, shall not be construed to deny or disparage others retained by the people.

Amendment X.

The powers not delegated to the United States by the Constitution, nor prohibited by it to the States, are reserved to the States respectively, or to the people.

AMENDMENTS 11-27

Amendment XI.

Passed by Congress March 4, 1794. Ratified February 7, 1795.

(Note: A portion of Article III, Section 2 of the Constitution was modified by the 11ᵗʰ Amendment.)

The Judicial power of the United States shall not be construed to extend to any suit in law or equity, commenced or prosecuted against one of the United States by Citizens of another State, or by Citizens or Subjects of any Foreign State.

Amendment XII.

Passed by Congress December 9, 1803. Ratified June 15, 1804.

(Note: A portion of Article II, Section 1 of the Constitution was changed by the 12th Amendment.)

The Electors shall meet in their respective states, and vote by ballot for President and Vice-President, one of whom, at least, shall not be an inhabitant of the same state with themselves; they shall name in their ballots the person voted for as President, and in distinct ballots the person voted for as Vice-President, and they shall make distinct lists of all persons voted for as President, and of all persons voted for as Vice-President, and of the number of votes for each, which lists they shall sign and certify, and transmit sealed to the seat of the government of the United States, directed to the President of the Senate;-the President of the Senate shall, in the presence of the Senate and House of Representatives, open all the certificates and the votes shall then be counted;-The person having the greatest number of votes for President, shall be the President, if such number be a majority of the whole number of Electors appointed; and if no person have such majority, then from the persons having the highest numbers not exceeding three on the list of those voted for as President, the House of Representatives shall choose immediately, by ballot, the President. But in choosing the President, the votes shall be taken by states, the representation from each state having one vote; a quorum for this purpose shall consist of a member or members from two-thirds of the states, and a majority of all the states shall be necessary to a choice. [And if the House of Representatives shall not choose a President whenever the right of choice shall devolve upon them, before the fourth day of March next following, then the Vice-President shall act as President, as in case of the death or other constitutional disability of the President.-]* The person having the greatest number of votes as Vice-President, shall be the Vice-President, if such number be a majority of the whole number of Electors appointed, and if no person have a majority, then from the two highest numbers on the list, the Senate shall choose the Vice-President; a quorum for the purpose shall consist of two-thirds of the whole number of Senators, and a majority of the whole number shall be necessary to a choice. But no person constitutionally ineligible to the office of President shall be eligible to that of Vice-President of the United States.

*Superseded by Section 3 of the 20th Amendment.

Amendment XIII.

Passed by Congress January 31, 1865. Ratified December 6, 1865.

(Note: A portion of Article IV, Section 2 of the Constitution was changed by the 13th Amendment.)

SECTION 1

Neither slavery nor involuntary servitude, except as a punishment for crime whereof the party shall have been duly convicted, shall exist within the United States, or any place subject to their jurisdiction.

SECTION 2

Congress shall have power to enforce this article by appropriate legislation.

Amendment XIV.

Passed by Congress June 13, 1866. Ratified July 9, 1868.

(Note: Article I, Section 2 of the Constitution was modified by Section 2 of the 14th Amendment.)

SECTION 1

All persons born or naturalized in the United States and subject to the jurisdiction thereof, are citizens of the United States and of the State wherein they reside. No State shall make or enforce any law which shall abridge the privileges or immunities of citizens of the United States; nor shall any State deprive any person of life, liberty, or property, without due process of law; nor deny to any person within its jurisdiction the equal protection of the laws.

SECTION 2

Representatives shall be apportioned among the several States according to their respective numbers, counting the whole number of persons in each State, excluding Indians not taxed. But when the right to vote at any election for the choice of electors for President and Vice President of the United States, Representatives in Congress, the Executive and Judicial officers of a State, or the members of the Legislature thereof, is denied to any of the male inhabitants of such State, [being twenty-one years of age,]* and citizens of the United States, or in any way abridged, except for participation in rebellion, or other crime, the basis of representation therein shall be reduced in the proportion which the number of such male citizens shall bear to the whole number of male citizens twenty-one years of age in such State.

SECTION 3

No person shall be a Senator or Representative in Congress, or elector of President and Vice President, or hold any office, civil or military, under the United States, or under any State, who, having previously taken an oath, as a member of Congress, or as an officer of the United States, or as a member of any State legislature, or as an executive or judicial officer of any State, to support the Constitution of the United States, shall have engaged in insurrection or rebellion against the same, or given aid or comfort to the enemies thereof. But Congress may by a vote of two-thirds of each House, remove such disability.

SECTION 4

The validity of the public debt of the United States, authorized by law, including debts incurred for payment of pensions and bounties for services in suppressing insurrection or rebellion, shall not be questioned. But neither the United States nor any State shall assume or pay any debt or obligation incurred in aid of insurrection or rebellion against the United States, or any claim for the loss or emancipation of any slave; but all such debts, obligations and claims shall be held illegal and void.

SECTION 5

The Congress shall have the power to enforce, by appropriate legislation, the provisions of this article.

*Changed by Section 1 of the 26th Amendment.

Amendment *XV.*

Passed by Congress February 26, 1869. Ratified February 3, 1870.

SECTION 1

The right of citizens of the United States to vote shall not be denied or abridged by the United States or by any State on account of race, color, or previous condition of servitude.

SECTION 2

The Congress shall have the power to enforce this article by appropriate legislation.

Amendment *XVI.*

Passed by Congress July 2, 1909. Ratified February 3, 1913.

(Note: Article I, Section 9 of the Constitution was modified by the 16^h Amendment.)

The Congress shall have power to lay and collect taxes on incomes, from whatever source derived, without apportionment among the several States, and without regard to any census or enumeration.

Amendment *XVII.*

Passed by Congress May 13, 1912. Ratified April 8, 1913.

(Note: Article I, Section 3 of the Constitution was modified by the 17th Amendment.)

The Senate of the United States shall be composed of two Senators from each State, elected by the people thereof, for six years; and each Senator shall have one vote. The electors in each State shall have the qualifications requisite for electors of the most numerous branch of the State legislatures.

When vacancies happen in the representation of any State in the Senate, the executive authority of such State shall issue writs of election to fill such vacancies: Provided, That the legislature of any State may empower the executive thereof to make temporary appointments until the people fill the vacancies by election as the legislature may direct.

This amendment shall not be so construed as to affect the election or term of any Senator chosen before it becomes valid as part of the Constitution.

Amendment *XVIII.*

Passed by Congress December 18, 1917. Ratified January 16, 1919. Repealed by the 21 Amendment, December 5, 1933.

SECTION 1

After one year from the ratification of this article the manufacture, sale, or transportation of intoxicating liquors within, the importation thereof into, or the exportation thereof from the United States and all territory subject to the jurisdiction thereof for beverage purposes is hereby prohibited.

SECTION 2

The Congress and the several States shall have concurrent power to enforce this article by appropriate legislation.

SECTION 3

This article shall be inoperative unless it shall have been ratified as an amendment to the Constitution by the legislatures of the several States, as provided in the Constitution, within seven years from the date of the submission hereof to the States by the Congress.

Amendment *XIX.*

Passed by Congress June 4, 1919. Ratified August 18, 1920.

The right of citizens of the United States to vote shall not be denied or abridged by the United States or by any State on account of sex.

Congress shall have power to enforce this article by appropriate legislation.

Amendment XX.

Passed by Congress March 2, 1932. Ratified January 23, 1933.

(Note: Article I, Section 4 of the Constitution was modified by Section 2 of this Amendment. In addition, a portion of the 12th Amendment was superseded by Section 3.)

SECTION 1

The terms of the President and the Vice President shall end at noon on the 20th day of January, and the terms of Senators and Representatives at noon on the 3d day of January, of the years in which such terms would have ended if this article had not been ratified; and the terms of their successors shall then begin.

SECTION 2

The Congress shall assemble at least once in every year, and such meeting shall begin at noon on the 3d day of January, unless they shall by law appoint a different day.

SECTION 3

If, at the time fixed for the beginning of the term of the President, the President elect shall have died, the Vice President elect shall become President. If a President shall not have been chosen before the time fixed for the beginning of his term, or if the President elect shall have failed to qualify, then the Vice President elect shall act as President until a President shall have qualified; and the Congress may by law provide for the case wherein neither a President elect nor a Vice President shall have qualified, declaring who shall then act as President, or the manner in which one who is to act shall be selected, and such person shall act accordingly until a President or Vice President shall have qualified.

SECTION 4

The Congress may by law provide for the case of the death of any of the persons from whom the House of Representatives may choose a President whenever the right of choice shall have devolved upon them, and for the case of the death of any of the persons from whom the Senate may choose a Vice President whenever the right of choice shall have devolved upon them.

SECTION 5

Sections 1 and 2 shall take effect on the 15th day of October following the ratification of this article.

SECTION 6

This article shall be inoperative unless it shall have been ratified as an amendment to the Constitution by the legislatures of three-fourths of the several States within seven years from the date of its submission.

Amendment XXI.

Passed by Congress February 20, 1933. Ratified December 5, 933.

SECTION 1

The eighteenth article of amendment to the Constitution of the United States is hereby repealed.

SECTION 2

The transportation or importation into any State, Territory, or possession of the United States for delivery or use therein of intoxicating liquors, in violation of the laws thereof, is hereby prohibited.

SECTION 3

This article shall be inoperative unless it shall have been ratified as an amendment to the Constitution by conventions in the several States, as provided in the Constitution, within seven years from the date of the submission hereof to the States by the Congress.

Amendment *XXII.*

Passed by Congress March 21, 1947. Ratified February 27, 951.

SECTION 1

No person shall be elected to the office of the President more than twice, and no person who has held the office of President, or acted as President, for more than two years of a term to which some other person was elected President shall be elected to the office of President more than once. But this Article shall not apply to any person holding the office of President when this Article was proposed by Congress, and shall not prevent any person who may be holding the office of President, or acting as President, during the term within which this Article becomes operative from holding the office of President or acting as President during the remainder of such term.

SECTION 2

This article shall be inoperative unless it shall have been ratified as an amendment to the Constitution by the legislatures of three-fourths of the several States within seven years from the date of its submission to the States by the Congress.

Amendment *XXIII.*

Passed by Congress June 16, 1960. Ratified March 29, 1961.

SECTION 1

The District constituting the seat of Government of the United States shall appoint in such manner as Congress may direct:

A number of electors of President and Vice President equal to the whole number of Senators and Representatives in Congress to which the District would be entitled if it were a State, but in no event more than the least populous State; they shall be in addition to those appointed by the States, but they shall be considered, for the purposes of the election of President and Vice President, to be electors appointed by a State; and they shall meet in the District and perform such duties as provided by the twelfth article of amendment.

SECTION 2

The Congress shall have power to enforce this article by appropriate legislation.

Amendment *XXIV.*

Passed by Congress August 27, 1962. Ratified January 23, 1964.

SECTION 1

The right of citizens of the United States to vote in any primary or other election for President or Vice President, for electors for President or Vice President, or for Senator or Representative in Congress, shall not be denied or abridged by the United States or any State by reason of failure to pay poll tax or other tax.

SECTION 2

The Congress shall have power to enforce this article by appropriate legislation.

Amendment *XXV.*

Passed by Congress July 6, 1965. Ratified February 10, 1967.
*(Note: Article II, Section 1 of the Constitution was modified by
the 25th Amendment.)*

SECTION 1

In case of the removal of the President from office or of
his death or resignation, the Vice President shall become
President.

SECTION 2

Whenever there is a vacancy in the office of the Vice President, the President shall nominate a Vice President who
shall take office upon confirmation by a majority vote of
both Houses of Congress.

SECTION 3

Whenever the President transmits to the President pro
tempore of the Senate and the Speaker of the House of
Representatives his written declaration that he is unable
to discharge the powers and duties of his office, and until
he transmits to them a written declaration to the contrary,
such powers and duties shall be discharged by the Vice
President as Acting President.

SECTION 4

Whenever the Vice President and a majority of either the
principal officers of the executive departments or of such
other body as Congress may by law provide, transmit to the
President pro tempore of the Senate and the Speaker of the
House of Representatives their written declaration that the
President is unable to discharge the powers and duties of
his office, the Vice President shall immediately assume the
powers and duties of the office as Acting President.

Thereafter, when the President transmits to the President
pro tempore of the Senate and the Speaker of the House of
Representatives his written declaration that no inability exists, he shall resume the powers and duties of his office unless the Vice President and a majority of either the principal
officers of the executive department or of such other body
as Congress may by law provide, transmit within four days
to the President pro tempore of the Senate and the Speaker
of the House of Representatives their written declaration
that the President is unable to discharge the powers and
duties of his office. Thereupon Congress shall decide the
issue, assembling within forty-eight hours for that purpose
if not in session. If the Congress, within twenty-one days
after receipt of the latter written declaration, or, if Congress
is not in session, within twenty-one days after Congress is
required to assemble, determines by two-thirds vote of both
Houses that the President is unable to discharge the powers
and duties of his office, the Vice President shall continue to
discharge the same as Acting President; otherwise, the President shall resume the powers and duties of his office.

Amendment *XXVI.*

Passed by Congress March 23, 1971. Ratified July 1, 1971.

*(Note: Amendment 14, Section 2 of the Constitution was
modified by Section 1 of the 26th Amendment.)*

SECTION 1

The right of citizens of the United States, who are eighteen
years of age or older, to vote shall not be denied or abridged
by the United States or by any State on account of age.

SECTION 2

The Congress shall have power to enforce this article by
appropriate legislation.

Amendment *XXVII.*

Originally proposed Sept. 25, 1789. Ratified May 7, 1992.

No law, varying the compensation for the services of the
Senators and Representatives, shall take effect, until an election of representatives shall have intervened.

The NCC is an independent, non-partisan, nonprofit organization that was established in 1988 under the Constitution Heritage Act. The Center's mission is to increase awareness and understanding of the Constitution, the Constitution's history and its relevance to people's daily lives.

National Constitution Center
525 Arch Street
Independence Mall
Philadelphia, PA 19106

(215) 409-6600
www.constitutioncenter.org